SEX,
LIES &
COOKIES

SEX,
LIES &
COOKIES

an unrated memoir

LISA G.

WILLIAM MORROW
An Imprint of HarperCollins*Publishers*

To my family, with love

FYI

Just so you know, names, identities, job descriptions, and any number of physical details of my numerous ex-boyfriends have been changed to protect the innocent. Or the not-so-innocent. If you are one of my ex-boyfriends and you think you recognize yourself in this book—don't be so sure that's you. Also, you should be flattered. Finally, I have smushed together some chronologies and changed the order of certain events just to keep things interesting. Believe me, it's better this way.

CONTENTS

Introduction   1

Chapter 1: Hello, This Is Lisa Glasberg   6
   Slice-and-Bake Chocolate Chip Cookies   18

Chapter 2: Confessions of a Type A Virgin   20
   Losing My Cherry Cookies   38

Chapter 3: Aunt Nina's Cookbook   40
   Meringue Kisses   44

Chapter 4: On-Air   45
   Chocolate Snowballs   55

Chapter 5: Married and Unavailable   56
   Gingerbread Men   69

Chapter 6: Sleepless in Manhattan   71
   Lisa Goes Nuts Brownies   91

Chapter 7: Fake 'n' Bake   93
    How-to-Get-a-Man Chocolate Chip   106
    Cheesecake Squares

Chapter 8: Cereal Monogamy   107
    Fruity Pebbles Cookies   117

Chapter 9: Love at First Sight   119
    Black-and-White Cookies   137

Chapter 10: If You Bake It, They Will Come   139
    Big Apple (Pie) Cookies   151

Chapter 11: What I Learned from TV   152
    Blondies   158

Chapter 12: Baker's Rack   159
    Double D-licious Oatmeal Cookies   166

Chapter 13: Why Can't You Get a Job Like Everyone Else?   167
    Linzer Broken-Heart Cookies   176

Chapter 14: In Case of Emergency, Break Glass   179
    Chocolate Therapy Chunk Cookies   190

Chapter 15: Late Bloomer   191
    Lemons-into-Lemonade Bars   204

Chapter 16: Getting Lucky   205
    Chocolate Chip Biscotti   219

Chapter 17: Perfect Is Boring   221
    Sugar Cookies   230

Epilogue (or, How You Too Can Be a
Cookie-Party-Throwing Goddess)   232

    Mini Apple Pies   252

    Plain-as-Butter Cookies   254

    Peppermint Bark Cookies   255

    Chocolate Sandwich Cookies with Vanilla Crème   256

    Thankful Cookies   257

    Green Tea Shortbread Cookies   258

    Diva Doodles (a.k.a. Snickerdoodles)   259

    Peanut Butter Cookies   260

    Chocolate Chow Mein Noodle Cookies   261

    Mudslides   261

    New Age Black-and-White Cookies   263

Acknowledgments   267

SEX,
LIES &
COOKIES

INTRODUCTION

I've had my heart crushed a few times. There's nothing like a man to reduce a strong woman to tears. But when I found true love—the kind of love that really breaks your heart—it wasn't in a relationship. It was in a job. That love was for real, and I cried when it was over the way I had never cried over a man.

I've wanted to be on the radio ever since I was old enough to turn the dial. I would lie in bed at night listening to the crackling voices floating out of the AM radio, dreaming of adding my voice to theirs—to have someone listen to me with the same kind of interest.

Maybe it's because I'm a middle child. We're attention seekers by nature. None of us believes we received as much notice as our older and younger siblings. Scratch a middle child and you'll find a well of insecurity. And I am pretty much a textbook example. I recently read there's even a psychiatric disorder called "Middle Child syndrome" that can actually result in psychotic behavior.

Just to answer two obvious questions you may now have:

1. No, I'm not psychotic.
2. Yes, I've checked with a professional.

Now you may wonder, why the radio? Why not move to Hollywood, like so many other wannabe starlets? First of all, I never had the kind of confidence in my own skin that I think most performers have. Not to mention, this was my idea of fashion:

That's right, my favorite outfit for many of my formative years was a very large pair of denim overalls. I wore them to death.

If I'd really wanted to be an actress, I suppose a good stylist could have addressed my fashion ineptitude. But showing myself off on-screen wasn't my interest. My three shining seasons performing with the Hewlett, Long Island, high school musicals were spent playing violin in the orchestra pit.

I didn't want to be seen—that was my perfect older sister's job (she was always the Marsha Brady to my Jan). No, I wanted to be *heard*. My voice—as Long Island Jewish as you could get—would be my fortune.

The nice thing about having people love you for your voice is that you don't have to be anywhere near them while they're listening to you. You can be far, far away. And that's how I liked it. Unfortunately, I carried that fear of intimacy into my personal life. I loved men, and I loved sex with men, but that whole relationship give-and-take thing? I wasn't such a fan of that. My idea of a giving relationship with a man was to bake him cookies and take them over to his apartment while wearing a fur coat and nothing underneath. And that's not giving—that's giving it away.

I made a lot of cookies during my days of romantic flailing around. And I had a lot of boyfriends, but none of them stuck. It took me a long time to figure out why: I'd spent my childhood compromising my wishes and feeling like I always came last. So as an adult I'd gone to the opposite extreme. To be happy, I thought that I had to come first, and I had to be heard *all* the time. Over time, I became so focused on being heard that I really didn't know how to listen.

My relationships suffered as a result, but hey, work was great! And that's nothing to sniff at. Men get rewarded for going after their careers single-mindedly. And if they get married at age forty-eight, and their wife happens to be fifteen years younger (so she's conveniently still well within her baby-making years), no one even raises an eyebrow. But if a woman spends decades on her career, doesn't get married, doesn't have kids . . . well, I don't need to tell you the kind of reaction that gets.

But I never felt like I'd missed out by following a less traditional route. I had a different dream, and I put my heart into achieving it. Then one day I realized that my dream had come true, but I needed something else—something more. And that something wasn't going to come from a guy or a job or anything else that I could chase or scratch off a list. That something had to come from inside of me—a place that I had been ignoring while I was so busy grasping for the brass ring in front of me.

Some people are born knowing the secret to happiness. The rest of us take a little longer, and we do a lot of living on our way to figuring things out. Call us the late bloomers. And this book is for us. We don't necessarily operate on the usual schedule or follow anyone else's tried-and-true formula. But what's the big hurry, anyway? Why is everyone in such a rush? If you have life all figured out by age twenty . . . or thirty . . . or even forty, what are you going to spend the rest of your life doing—knitting? Watching TV? Personally, I think trial and error is a lot more interesting than knowing how your life is going to look before you've even lived it yet. Some of the best cookie recipes I've ever invented were the result of a few massive failures on the way to figuring out the right formula. We late bloomers are like that. And we're worth the wait—and the trial and error. Because once we hit on that magic combination of ingredients, we're delicious.

CHAPTER 1

HELLO, THIS IS LISA GLASBERG

My parents have three daughters—my older sister, Bonnie; middle child, me; and my younger sister, Andrea—and they love all of us. But my parents, who didn't divorce until I was already out of the house, definitely did not love each other. As a result, my whole childhood and young adulthood were colored by their bickering. Our home was not a happy one. So it's no wonder I never wanted to get married. When my friends would fantasize about their eventual wedding day, I would look at them like they were crazy. I couldn't even compute the desire to get married—based on what I knew of marriage, why would anyone want that?

Because my home wasn't a place of comfort for me, I sought distraction elsewhere. I spent most of my time outside, burning off my endless amounts of nervous energy. I spent a lot of time at my friend Jeanie's house, becoming like a fourth daughter in her family. And I threw myself into a multitude of activities at school, from clubs to sports to Girl Scouts. Most of all, I loved the violin.

My music teachers gave me the positive feedback I craved. They seemed to really get me. They didn't judge me by how I looked or fit in with their preconceived expectations. They judged me for my work, period. And with hard work, they told me, I could accomplish something amazing. To this day, this is one of the biggest things I love about music, and why I think it's so important for kids to have music in their lives. Positive results in music are all about practice and persistence—it doesn't matter what anyone thinks of you in any other context. If you work hard at your instrument, you get better—it's as easy and honest as that. So I worked hard. I treasured my violin, and I practiced, and I performed in concerts. By high school I was in our orchestra's first section, and I made second violin in the All-State Orchestra.

The violin was something I did for my own enjoyment—it was all my own. And that was really important to me, especially since I felt like an alien species in my own home. Of course the world is at least 50 percent populated by people who felt like freaks growing up, but that doesn't make it any less painful when you're going through it yourself. My father and I didn't communicate well when I was

younger—now things have changed, and as an adult
I've grown to appreciate him for who he is, and vice
versa. He's become a really great listener, and I've
grown more thankful for how well he always took
care of us. But back then, it felt different. A former marine (yes, a Jewish marine), he dealt with his
household full of females—even our dogs and cats
were girls—by receding or laying down the law. If
you take a look at pictures of my intimidatingly fit
father then and now, you'll not only understand why
I didn't lose my virginity until college, you might
also wonder how I ever managed to lose it at all.

My dad, age 20.

My dad, age 84.

Meanwhile my mother and my older sister, Bonnie, were a twosome. The two of them spoke the same language, and I was a foreigner with no glossary or clue to the underlying meanings. They even had the same fashion sense. Right or wrong, I felt like Bonnie was the golden girl and I was the weird ugly duckling. I couldn't help feeling that my mother would love me more if only I were more like my sister.

I remember one time when my mother asked each of us girls what special thing we might like from the grocery store. Bonnie asked for blackout cake, which happened to be my mother's favorite as well. I asked for slice-and-bake cookies. I'm not sure what Andrea asked for, but that's her story to tell. Inevitably, my mother came back from the store with blackout cake and no slice-and-bake cookies. She brushed the oversight aside and said she just forgot. But I couldn't even hide my disappointment. How could she forget something so simple, and after she'd made a point of asking me what I wanted? It was a small thing, and I know my mother didn't mean to hurt my feelings, but the memory has stuck with me. Then and always the message came through to me loud and clear: I could speak, but no one was listening. Is it any wonder that I went into radio?

MY DAD GREW UP outside of Boston, a six-foot-three football player with thick dark hair and blue eyes.

He met my mother on a blind date. She was just as irresistible in her own way—five foot seven, she modeled and acted in college and had a gamine Audrey Hepburn look. This was just one more way that my mother and I were completely different from each other. I would end up taking after my busty grandmothers and I barely hit five feet, three inches (I suspect this is because in every picture I've ever seen of my mom pregnant, she's holding a glass of wine in one hand and a cigarette in the other just like a character out of *Mad Men*, but it's just a theory).

As gorgeous as my parents were as a couple, emotionally they were a disaster together. And they knew it, too. I look back on it now, and as miserable as it often was to grow up in that household, I feel genuinely bad for them. They must have felt so trapped in their misery. I found out years later that they wanted to separate after my older sister, Bonnie, was born, but all four of their parents laid down the law and insisted that they stay together. And that's how an already-unhappy couple brings two more children into the world. I know they were glad to have all of us, but it couldn't have been easy for either of them.

It must have been especially overwhelming for my mother to have three kids in short succession, and to be stuck in a loveless marriage. My dad was a good breadwinner, but the money came with steel strings attached—he paid the bills, so he expected to set the rules. I think that's why I always wanted to pay my own bills as an adult—I never wanted any man to make the rules for me or feel that his contribution to my fiscal well-being meant that I owed him in some way. But I'm getting ahead of myself.

My dad hugely expanded his family's import business, which meant that he traveled all the time and also worked long hours in the city. While he was away on his trips, things were relatively calm at home. Not necessarily happy, but calm. The tension would gradually build when he was expected home, though. We'd all wonder when the screaming would start up again. Would it be right as he walked through the door, or would something tick him off later? Would my mother say something cutting, or would he criticize her? My sisters and I tiptoed around them or fled to our rooms to wait out the storm when it hit. We very rarely ate together as a family, even at dinnertime. Who could stomach it?

I think that's why my high school yearbook entry looked like this:

"No act of kindness, no matter how small, is ever wasted."

Yearbook 9–12; Editor in Chief 12
Cheerleading 9; Captain 10, 11;
Co-Captain 12

Student Council 9, 10; Class VP 11, 12
Tennis team 10–12
Orchestra 9–12
Student Faculty Rapport 10–11
Play 9–11
Carnival 10–12
Ambition: To be able to say "Hello, this is Lisa
Glasberg, WLIR FM, 92.7."

It kills me now to look back on how busy I was. I grabbed any excuse to get out of the house, to distract myself with people and activity. How did I have time to eat or sleep? That pattern of overworking (and overplaying) wouldn't let up for years. It was no coincidence that I eventually chose a profession with crazy hours and little downtime. I was never good at being quiet and contemplative. In fact, the only time I was truly still was when I was listening to the radio.

When I was thirteen and my parents finished our attic, I took it as my bedroom—because I couldn't get farther away than that without moving out. It was hot and stuffy up there, but I painted the walls yellow and I loved it. In my own private space, I could press my ear to my little AM radio and lose myself. Late at night in my bedroom, when the rest of the house was asleep, was when I could get the best signals from faraway radio stations. Hearing a radio station all the way from Buffalo was as exciting to me as a trip to Europe would be for a normal person. The radio was my first love, and other than the violin, it was my only true, passionate love.

Radio made everything bearable. When my dad woke us all up at 4 A.M. on a freezing, pitch-black Saturday morning to go skiing with him, the car radio was what I looked forward to. These ski trips were nonnegotiable, no matter how bitterly miserable we were. I still remember how my father would simultaneously knock and open the doors to our bedrooms, booming, "Time to get up! Let's go!" We'd groan and throw the covers over our heads, but he wouldn't take whining for an answer. We'd be out the door in five minutes, and I was the fastest because I'd always lay out all my clothes the night before—a habit I kept up when I started working in morning radio.

Once we were in the car, my dad would immediately tune the radio to talk or news, and I'd start begging for music instead. (*Please, Dad, can't we listen to the Beatles?*) Finally we came up with a compromise. He could listen to talk radio on the way there, but then on the way back he'd let me listen to WABC with Cousin Brucie and Dan Ingram. I soaked it up like a sponge, and for a little while I could have been anywhere—definitely not in the backseat of my parents' car crammed next to my sisters.

I truly think radio saved my life, because it gave me a path to get to a life of my own. My high school had a work-study program for seniors, and I vividly remember the day the guest speaker was a DJ from WLIR. I made a beeline for him once his talk was over, and I asked if they had an internship program. He handed me the program director's card, and I raced home to call him for an interview.

The WLIR studio was in Garden City, Long Island, so I drove there (newly licensed) in the big clunk of an Oldsmobile I'd inherited from my grandparents. That car looked like a boat, it sounded like a boat, and even then it was old. But it had an AM radio that I'd jury-rigged with an FM radio that hung from the dashboard by a wire, and that was all that mattered to me. My chosen interview outfit was a polyester Huckapoo shirt and high-waisted bell-bottoms. Despite my fashion sense, Ken Cole, the station director, hired me on the spot.

As much as I had fantasized about working for a radio station, even I had to admit that local radio wasn't glamorous—I remember bad wood paneling and a strip mall location that would have been the perfect setting for an axe murder. The interior looked like a barely finished attic (ah, just like home). The walls were covered in cork bulletin boards with random postings of events around Long Island. And it had the particular smell that all local radio stations have—a little musty, a little electrical. The equipment was set up on big rolling carts and looked like something out of a cheap science fiction movie, with massive knobs and toggle switches. The stylus for the turntable was as big as the leg of a couch. I remember being transfixed by the skill with which the DJ could turn down the volume so you couldn't hear the scratching while he cued up the next record. It was like magic to me.

I had my own little cubicle, and I worked under the news director writing public service announcements. At least at the start, I kept my mouth shut. I was terrified of looking stupid. I pictured asking my boss a question, and him realizing: *Oh my God, I hired a moron.* So I kept my lips sealed, my eyes and ears wide open, and I soaked up as much knowledge as I could.

As scared as I was to make a mistake, the guys on staff—all of them with faces made for radio— were an incredibly nice bunch of misfits. They were either unkempt, or overweight, or gave new meaning to the word *hairy.* In some cases they were all of the above. And I fit right in by being just as much of a misfit in my own way. From them I learned that radio stations are ready-made families. But unlike in my own family, there was no odd man out, because *everyone* was odd. What an amazing feeling that was, to be instantly and thoroughly accepted. Radio was the perfect environment for an outcast like me (it still is).

I knew that being on the radio wasn't the most typical aspiration for a high school girl, but I was always good at keeping up with all the activities that a high school girl was supposed to do—like cheerleading—so I never gave my parents or classmates a reason to think that I was such a freak of nature. I was really social and I played along with expectations, but while my girlfriends were all putting a lot of energy into their boyfriends and who they were dating, I couldn't have cared less about getting a boyfriend. They were happily ensconced in high school and wondering who would be voted prom queen, but I was already set to fly the coop.

I was living two separate lives—my typical high school life, and my radio life. And this compartmentalizing of personal life and career aspirations would be a pattern that I would repeat for years. It was only much later in my life that I learned that it's possible to integrate both sides of yourself into one healthy personality. Back then I thought I had to put 100 percent of myself into radio if I was going to succeed in achieving my dream.

Maintaining my two separate lives was exhausting. It's impossible to be fully present in any part of your life when you're split in two, so I was constantly jerking back and forth between my two worlds. I wore my popular high school girl costume when I was at school, and then I put on my career costume when I went to the radio station. And I danced as fast I could between both worlds, always a frenzy of activity and striving. I joke now that if they'd had that show *So You Think You Can*

Dance back then, I might not have won for talent, but I definitely would have gotten a prize for sheer manic energy.

My first on-air assignment for WLIR was making a public service announcement geared at high schoolers. My bit wasn't long, it wasn't even interesting, but my voice was on the radio, and that meant that people were listening to me. The power! I still have the recording, so trust that I am not exaggerating when I say that I sounded like Long Island Lolita Amy Fisher (and that's never a good thing). Here's an excerpt, phonetically rendered so you can get the full humorous impact:

> *Woodjoo like something that is priceless, at no cawst ta you? Then register to vote during ya high school votah registration droive in Mahch. Thell be tables set up. Look fa dem.*

Listening to it now, I especially love the way I overpronounced certain words, such as "register." I was trying *so* hard to sound like a professional. Then the strain obviously became too much for me, and by the end of my spiel I was full on Long Island Lolita again.

Okay, so it wasn't a great start, but it was a start. I'd lost my radio virginity. I wasn't even legal to drink yet, and my high school yearbook ambition had already come true.

When I was a kid growing up in Long Island, the best food came in a wrapper. Why cook from scratch when you could have Yankee Doodles cold from the fridge, or Fritos from a bag? And how about the true nirvana of all convenience foods, slice-and-bake cookies from a tube? Truth be told, I still love them, but here's my from-scratch version of the original. They give you a nice flashback to childhood, but they're so much more delicious than the ones you remember.

P.S., when baking cookies, don't let them brown too much. My cookie mantra is: when in doubt, pull out (after all, have you ever heard anyone complain about an underdone chocolate chip cookie?). Then, once the cookies are set (about a minute after you remove them from the oven), transfer them to a baking rack to finish cooling.

SLICE-AND-BAKE CHOCOLATE CHIP COOKIES

1 cup (2 sticks) unsalted butter, softened
1¼ cups packed light brown sugar
¼ cup granulated sugar
2 eggs
1 teaspoon vanilla

2¼ cups all-purpose flour
½ teaspoon baking soda
12 ounces semisweet chocolate chips
Parchment paper for rolling up the dough
Parchment-lined cookie sheets

Preheat oven to 350 degrees.

Using an electric mixer, cream together softened butter and sugars. Scrape down sides of bowl. Mix in eggs and vanilla until incorporated. In a small bowl, stir together flour and baking soda, then blend into butter mixture. Fold in chocolate chips.

Divide dough into two batches. Tear off a long sheet (about 18 inches or so) of parchment paper and place sideways on the counter. Now scoop one half of the dough onto the paper about one-third from the bottom of the sheet and use your hands to form the dough into a rough log. Using the top (long side) of the paper, fold the paper over the dough and gently push while squeezing (with your palm) to form a smooth log. Keep squeezing until the dough is 3 inches in diameter and 12 inches long (feel free to let your imagination run wild while doing this—it keeps things interesting). Square off the edges by pushing in the ends with your palms. Now do the same with the other half of the dough.

Chill both logs in the refrigerator for about 30 minutes, or until the dough is firm and sliceable.

When firm, take sharp knife and cut ¼-inch slices. Because these don't have all the lovely artificial ingredients that help to hold together the store-bought slice-and-bake cookies, you might find that these crumble a bit around the edges as you slice them. If they do, don't sweat it. Just smush them back together again. Once they're baked, I promise you: no one will care. As you slice, space the rounds 2 inches apart on the parchment-lined cookie sheets.

Bake 12 to 15 minutes or until cookies are golden at the edges.

Makes around 48 cookies.

> **Note:** If you don't want to make both logs at once, you
> can always freeze one for using later. There's nothing like a
> warm chocolate chip cookie, so it's great to have a log of
> these handy when the craving hits. Just slice off as much
> as you want and store the rest.

CHAPTER 2

CONFESSIONS OF
A TYPE A VIRGIN

Once I started my internship at WLIR, I became as single-minded as that female GPS voice that won't let you even think about taking a different route. I had a few months of high school left, but I was just biding my time until graduation. Nothing could distract me from my goal of a career in radio. You could try to turn me in a different direction, but I'd always find my way back again.

I was so career obsessed that I wasn't even all that excited about my high school prom, as perhaps you can tell from the haphazard outfit I chose for the occasion. I don't recall putting even the slightest thought into what I'd be wearing, and, yeah, it shows.

The guy I went with was perfectly nice, but this was not a love match, and that was exactly the way I wanted it. In fact, I asked him out because we were friends—*just* friends. Here I was, seventeen years old, my last year of high school, and I should have been all gooey-eyed and excited about the prom, the BIG NIGHT (a.k.a. the occasion upon which you lose your virginity to your high school boyfriend). But that wasn't on my agenda. I just wanted to go to the damn prom, get it over with, graduate, and then move on.

I was ready to move past the whole world that I'd been living in but that felt so disconnected from me as a person. I wasn't cut out for spending weekends at the mall or the country club. I couldn't really relate to the kids who got a Mercedes-Benz for a birthday gift, and whose parents bragged about which Ivy League school they were going to. I had never aspired to any of that.

I definitely wasn't like the spoiled beautiful girls at school who seemed to sail through life on their good looks. I'd gotten the message from both my parents that my looks were not going to get me far in life. My father had even suggested that I consider getting a nose job. I was a teenager and I think we were sitting at the dinner table at the time. And my mother would take one look at me and just roll her eyes. Recalling it now, I can't blame her, because it must be incredibly frustrating to look at your daughter and know she'd be better off if she only took your advice. It was your typical mother-daughter adolescent battle, and I decided that if I couldn't please her—and I couldn't be her—then why even try? So I gave up and decided to focus on other things. I had below-sea-level self-esteem, but I didn't know any different. I just plodded along, and I figured that my appearance wasn't my strong suit. I certainly didn't let it get me down or hold me back. I always did a good job of fitting in at school, and I had tons of friends that I still have today.

Still, all the while that I was smiling and nodding to the outside world, on the inside my career clock was ticking, and my bags were figuratively packed. I chose Hofstra for college not because it was close to home (no way), but because I already had a foot in the door in local radio. It was also close to the city, where all the best radio stations were—New York radio was the Emerald City at the end of my own personal yellow brick road. Another mark in Hofstra's favor was that it had a campus radio station where I started working within minutes of arriving on campus.

While I was there, I was never really *there*. I never gave myself a chance to be goofy and aimless, to shop around for a major—or a boyfriend. I never just kicked back with friends and philosophized and expressed inane opinions that would embarrass me later or took crazy road trips (or acid trips). I was so focused on my goals that I treated everything I did like an item on my mental to-do list. And while some of the items were way more important than others, I was equally methodical about crossing each one off. This is what my typical list looked like:

1. Practice violin
2. Study for statistics midterm
3. Lose Amy Fisher accent
4. Return library books
5. Buy more Cup-a-Soup
6. Lose virginity

By far, the last item on the list was my biggest issue. I'd spent my last year of high school without the slightest concern for crossing that milestone. But now that I was in college, my intact hymen was getting just a little embarrassing. This was the free love '70s after all, but if my actionless dorm room was any indication, it might as well have been the '50s . . . the *1850s*.

It was a lot easier to focus on the other items on my list, so I decided that I really needed to deal with my voice. No one on the radio sounded like me. The

DJs I listened to—the ones I wanted to be—definitely didn't mutilate their vowels the way I did. If I were starting out today, my thick *Lon Gisland* accent might have been an asset, but back then the ideal was to sound neutral. Since my career was the most important thing in the world to me, I decided that this self-improvement goal was much higher priority than losing my virginity. I could keep my sex life (or lack thereof) to myself, but there was no way I was going to get more airtime if I couldn't tawk bettah. At the first opportunity I took a speech class, and I became the Henry Higgins to my own Eliza Doolittle. I spent hours and hours in the college listening lab. Instead of studying my French tapes like I should have for my intermediate French class, I snuck in my own on-air reels to listen to how I sounded, where my vowels and consonants went wrong, and how I could correct them.

The funny thing is that all the while I was trying to sound neutral, the person I really emulated was Barbara Walters. And who sounds more distinctive than her? I was really struck by her career. Number one, she was a famous woman in broadcast, which was still very much a man's world. And number two, she was an interviewer who was just as famous as her subjects. That was my dream.

About a year after I started at Hofstra, I got my first paying job at a radio station, working for WBAB in Babylon, New York. I was eighteen years old, and I already felt like an adult. I'd never been your typical coed, but this was really the start of my life being all about work. I went to classes in the morning, then I worked at the radio station in the afternoon and evening. I had no social life to distract me. It never even occurred to me that I was missing out on campus parties and events. None of my high school friends had ended up at Hofstra with me, and with the exception of my roommate I had no other college friends who might have tried to lure me away from work for a few hours. I was always such a moving target—I'd never sit still long enough for anyone to be friendly with me. My closest friends (and they weren't that close) were the people I worked with at the station and the musicians I met along the way. A pattern had officially been set in place: my work and my social life were one and the same.

If WLIR looked like the setting for an axe murder, then WBAB's studio looked like the undiscovered location of a serial killing. It was really just a ranch house out on Route 109, with thick shag carpeting of an unidentifiable color. I shudder to think what one of those UV lights that they use at crime scenes would have turned up on those surfaces. If Dexter were the overnight DJ, he would have gone unnoticed.

WBAB consisted of two separate stations while I was there—the FM music station, and the AM Christian gospel station. In those days, the FCC required all stations to broadcast a certain amount of news at regular intervals throughout the day. It didn't matter what your main programming was, you also had to have someone doing newscasts. And that someone was me—even for the Christian gospel station. But my job for the Christian station was a little different, because after I did my on-air newscast, I also had to read a Bible verse. There I was, a nice Jewish girl from Long Island (my pronunciation had already improved!) and I had my own "Jesus File." At least that's what I called it. Every broadcast, after I'd read the news, I'd pull a little card from the front of the file, and on it was my Bible reading for the day. I'll never forget this choice passage from the New Testament:

> *He who believes in Jesus is not condemned; he who does not believe is condemned already, because he has not believed in the name of the only Son of God.*

I was such a hard worker, and such a believer in doing what your employer told you to do, that it never would have occurred to me to object. And that which does not kill you gives you a story to tell later.

That radio station specialized in some strange programming. My direct boss, Joel Martin, hosted a UFO show on Sunday nights. Listeners would call in from all over and they'd describe the Frisbee or whatever it was that had just sailed through their backyard and that they swore was an alien visitor. It was pretty odd, but it didn't bother me at all. And I wasn't even slightly perturbed that Joel was the news director and yet he engaged in serious conversations about paranormal activity. Joel was just one in a series of peculiar, awesome characters I worked with in radio. I'm pretty convinced that all the sort-of normal people in broadcast—the ones with a little more caution about how they looked and sounded—went over to TV. The rest of us less-photogenic types stuck with radio. And as ever, that was fine by me.

NOW WE MUST GET back to the whole virginity thing. It was time to lose it—even I had to admit that. With the clock ticking, and determined not to enter my twenties a virgin, I went about the task of giving it up in my usual methodical way: step by step. The first issue was to identify who I should have sex with. I immediately decided on Barry, a guy I'd worked with at the college radio station. He was nice, and he liked me more than I liked him so I wasn't worried about getting emotionally involved. I also had a feeling he would respect my privacy. He wasn't a big talker, so he wouldn't be looking for me to open up and tell him my life story. He was perfect on all counts.

The next issue was where to do it. My prison cell of a dorm room was the safest bet, since I wanted to be on home turf.

Finally, I needed to pick the background music: I settled on my favorite album at the time—Stevie Wonder's *Fulfillingness' First Finale*.

A different sort of girl might also have planned out what she was going to wear to the seduction of the century, but I was the same old Lisa I ever was, and changing my clothes really didn't occur to me. God only knows what underwear I had on. I'm sure Eve's fig leaf was silkier than whatever bloomers I was wearing. Not that it would have mattered to Barry—I really don't think he was expecting expensive lingerie.

After planning out all the particulars, I didn't waste any more time. After all, I had a to-do list to get back to. So the next time that Barry and I were in the campus pub, I turned to him and said, "Hey, wanna come up to my room?"

I'm sure his chin dropped a bit, but he wasn't one to look a gift horse in the mouth. He dutifully followed me back to my eight-foot-by-eight-foot cell, and the seduction began in earnest.

"Nice poster," he said, looking up at my massive poster of The Who, with sexy Roger Daltry front and center.

"Thanks," I said, while oh so elegantly sweeping the accumulation of junk off my purple bedspread. "Have a seat."

He did. Then he glanced around. "Nice room."

I looked at my white walls and linoleum floor

and figured he was just being polite. "When I'm a big-time DJ, I'm gonna have shag carpeting," I said.

"Cool," Barry said. That one word seemed to have tapped out his conversational abilities and he went silent after that.

Then I lit the candle by my bed—the one I'd stuck in a bottle of Chianti with wax running down the sides. The music was on, the runway was clear, the lighting was just right, and now it was time to get to work.

I sat down next to him, leaned in for a kiss, and didn't waste any time. Within seconds, off came his rock T-shirt and overalls (I said he worked in campus radio, didn't I?), and my jeans and peasant blouse (ditto) quickly followed.

I was trying to play it like I knew what I was doing, but I had no idea. I thought I would just follow his lead, but as it turned out, he didn't know up from down either. It's a good thing we were so young and flexible, because otherwise we really could have hurt ourselves. Instead of moving sinuously to the sweet sounds of Stevie Wonder, we looked more like we were square dancing to a skipping record.

Poor Barry. At one point I actually asked him, "Is it in?" It wasn't.

Then, finally, it was. While Barry pumped away on top of me, I lay back and looked up at Roger Daltry.

Minutes later, it was over. And at that point I thought to myself exactly what women the world over have thought to themselves in precisely the same situation: *So that's it? What's all the fuss about?*

But the deed was done—yay! Now I could revise my to-do list:

1. Practice violin
2. Avoid Barry
3. Shave legs (maybe I should have done that before I had sex with Barry?)
4. Avoid Barry
5. Buy more Cup-a-Soup
6. Avoid Barry

I THOUGHT I WAS so in control—I had it all figured out. Sex was no big deal, and my dream career was a light at the end of the tunnel, getting brighter all the time. What else was there to do but keep on charging ahead? I was on top of the world.

Let's take a significant pause right here. Dim the lights, and enter Joe, stage right. This is the man who taught Lisa that she wasn't nearly as in control as she thought she was. (Why am I speaking in the third person, you ask? Because it seemed more dramatic that way.)

I was nineteen, he was thirty-three. I met him at a Manhattan radio station where I interned one summer in college. He knew everyone in the business and got invited to all the best parties. We flirted and flirted, and then flirted some more. Sometimes we flirted in the office, sometimes over drinks—and more drinks. Was he good-looking? No, not really. Was he already living with someone else? Oh, yes he was.

I remember exactly how I found out. Joe and I were out at a bar with a lot of other people at the station, and at a certain point he leaned into me very close, and he said, "You know, Lisa, I have a girlfriend."

The way he said it to me, it was almost like he thought it would be a turn-on. And I'm ashamed to say this now, but actually . . . it was. As low as my self-esteem was at the time, I was flattered that he was with me instead of his girlfriend. Some people say that they have a little voice inside of them that talks to them at moments when they need to make a critical decision. I don't have a little voice, though; I have a ticker tape, like the old Associated Press wire that every radio station had in those days shooting out the top headlines. Right now, my ticker tape read, *News flash: Someone is paying attention to you, Lisa. That must mean that you're worth something!* On top of it, the guy who was with me was choosing to be with me *instead* of someone else that he really should be with. That must mean that I was *really* worth something!

I must have gone quiet for a second while the ticker tape was running in my head, because Joe looked at me meaningfully and said, "You know how it is."

Of course I had no idea "how it is." I was barely

nineteen. But I nodded like I was a sophisticated woman of the world who'd been around the block at least a few times.

Then he added the kicker. "We've got an open relationship. She knows I need my space."

I should have been disgusted, and now I would tell him that he was full of crap, but back then I was complimented by the attention. It's so pathetic how little he gave me, and how happy it made me. It's not like he was taking me out somewhere nice and showing me off or declaring any kind of public affection for me. We were in a totally unromantic Midtown bar where office workers went for some liquid courage before hitting the commuter rails. This place was most definitely off-peak—which made me Joe's off-peak girlfriend. But I was so delusional that I saw this as a huge romantic conquest.

Now let's pause for another moment. Why, you are surely asking yourself, did I continue with a guy like that? In my defense, did you also wonder how that chick Anastasia could be such a pushover for that guy Christian Grey? In response to both questions I can only say: youth and stupidity are powerful aphrodisiacs. And for some, money is, too. Christian, after all, is filthy rich. So maybe Anastasia's not so stupid.

But back to my point: Joe was no Christian Grey, and he definitely wasn't showering me with gifts, but I was no less addicted than Anastasia. It didn't matter to me that Joe looked like a lost Doobie Brother—the one who couldn't sing and was put up for adoption at puberty. Joe had more than enough confidence for both of us. He was the kind of man who saw exactly what he wanted when he looked in the mirror, and he liked what he saw. He swaggered with deejay power in my small world. He had actually met Jefferson Starship. I thought he was worldly.

Our dates were conducted in a haze of gin and tonic, his drink of choice. He was twice my size and age, so when I say that I tried to keep up with him drink for drink, I hope you get the full picture of how wasted I'd be by the end of the night. In that inebriated state it didn't take long before we'd move past making out in the bar to sex in his car.

I guess at the time I convinced myself that this was passion, but bear in mind that we weren't parked in a secluded make-out point out of some 1950s movie. This was 1970s Manhattan, when the crime statistics were through the roof. If I was going to end up as a line item on the police blotter, then the risk I was taking should have been worth it. I was putting my very life on the line for an orgasm, while transvestite hookers and drug dealers plied their trade a few feet away. I could be screaming with excitement or fear, and who would know the difference?

Now I just shake my head that I took all those chances for great sex, because truth be told, how good can sex really be in the back of a car? It's one of those things that sounds so much better than it is. We'd end up twisted into such tight pretzels that we'd need the jaws of life to separate us. It was horrible—I felt like I was in a bad game of Twister. My back hurt, I was sweating, and at least a few times I ripped out a clump of my long hair in the metal ashtray. After it was all over I looked like an extra in a zombie movie, with unkempt hair and blotched mascara under my eyes. Then, while I was still barely sober enough to stand, my so-called knight in shining armor dumped me onto the Long Island Railroad for my long trip back home. We've all heard of the walk of shame. I had the ride of shame—ten local stops and an hour's worth of pity stares from the conductor.

Thirty years later this doesn't sound so appealing—it was typical *Smart Women, Foolish Choices*-type stuff. But back then it was beyond hot to me. The fact that he was older and unavailable (Hi, Daddy Issues? This is me, Lisa) heightened everything to a crazy degree. I was hooked. And this became a pattern that would repeat itself for years. All he had to do was crook a little finger and I came running. He took me out of my insulated college world and into coked-up Manhattan parties and handed me VIP backstage passes to rock concerts. What wasn't to love? For the first time, I felt attractive and special. This was monumental for me. It was a constant high.

Until it wasn't. Because, of course, I wasn't the only girl he was drinking gin and tonics with.

I already knew about the live-in girlfriend—who was a six-foot-tall amazon, mind you—but I guess I thought I was the only one *in addition* to her. Plus, Joe made me laugh, which is a very attractive quality in any man, and he knew everything (I thought) about the business we both loved. I remember he called me "the Hawk," which had something to do with my devotion to the news and felt much more like a term of endearment than it sounds. Beyond our quick, furtive sex and the occasional professional pat on the head, it never dawned on me to ask for more than the crumbs he was giving me. I didn't feel I had the right to. Instead, I tried to act cool, and I pretended to like Foghat because he did.

It was all so pathetic, and I think on some level I came to realize it. I didn't really want to be this sad sack of a girl, desperate for a man's attention. I longed to be like Alison Steele, the beautiful red-headed deejay I loved to listen to. She had a gorgeous, smoky voice and a huge following as "the Nightbird." She'd begin her show every night by reciting poetry over New Agey music before murmuring her sultry introduction:

> *The flutter of wings, the shadow across the moon, the sounds of the night, as the Nightbird spreads her wings and soars, above the earth, into another level of comprehension, where we exist only to*

feel. Come, fly with me, Alison Steele, the
Nightbird, at WNEW-FM, until dawn.

The Nightbird played long uninterrupted sets of progressive rock, albums from groups like Tangerine Dream. She was edgy, mysterious, alluring. So unlike me.

Once I discovered how unspecial I was to Joe, and how many other girls he was sleeping with, things still dragged on awhile longer. My work at the station continued, and Joe was part of the social scene that I wanted to be a part of too. So I hung on.

Then, I graduated. And then, *it* happened. I got the call. A big FM station in Chicago was flipping over to a rock format. The program director wanted to know if I was interested in a real, full-time newsperson job.

"I can start Monday," I answered.

I told Joe my news over the phone.

"We can still see each other," he said. Maybe he'd drop in on me in Chicago, he suggested, or we could hook up when I came home for the holidays. I said something vague about needing to get settled and left it at that.

The only person who wasn't surprised by how quickly I could turn my back on the past was me. Everyone else seemed shocked that I could drop everything and move to a city I'd never even been to. Joe was certainly shocked. But I was done with him, just like I was done with college. Now real life started.

My mother was concerned, as any parent would be. She would have felt better if I'd had at least one nice, Jewish girlfriend in Chicago so I wouldn't be totally alone. And my girlfriends were worried about me, too, but they were too involved in their own lives to give it too much thought. They were at that stage of figuring out where they stood with their boyfriends, and trying to wrangle proposals. Meanwhile, the only proposal I cared about was from a radio station. (WMET: "Will you, Lisa Glasberg, devote your entire life to being on the radio?" Me: "I will!") A microphone and headset were the equivalent of my engagement ring and wedding band.

Before I could start this new chapter of my life and move myself to Chicago, I had to shed some stuff. I've never been one to become attached to things, so I had no problem giving away pretty much everything I owned—even my beloved violin. I told myself that there would be no time to practice anymore . . . so why have it? I gave it away to a quirky guy I knew who'd always wanted to play.

"Are you sure?" he asked me.

"Just take it!" I insisted, wanting the separation to be over as quickly as possible. "Just take it and go!"

I felt like a little kid trying to convince my dog that I didn't love him anymore. But I couldn't afford that kind of sentiment—it was radio or bust. All or nothing. No looking back at Old Yeller.

Losing my virginity may not have been such a thrill, but I promise you: these cookies never disappoint. And isn't that more than you can say for any number of ex-boyfriends? Whenever I make drop cookies like these I use my secret weapon. It's the size 100 (³/₈-ounce) ice cream scoop. It makes the perfect-sized cookie for entertaining and leaves your guests (and boyfriends) wanting more. The cookies are small enough to pop in your mouth in one gulp, and who can stop at one?

LOSING MY CHERRY COOKIES

¾ cup (1½ sticks) unsalted butter, at room temperature
½ cup sugar
½ teaspoon vanilla
1¾ cup all-purpose flour
1 cup semisweet chocolate chips
4 tablespoons milk

2 10-ounce jars maraschino cherries, drained, 2 teaspoons cherry juice, reserved

Parchment-lined cookie sheets

Preheat oven to 350 degrees.

Using an electric handheld or standing mixer, combine butter and sugar until fluffy. Scrape down the sides of the bowl, then add vanilla and mix again. Slowly add flour and mix until just combined.

Chill dough in the refrigerator for about 15 minutes.

Meanwhile, in a small saucepan (on very low heat), melt the chocolate and milk until smooth, stirring constantly. Alternatively, you can melt the chocolate and milk in a microwave set to high for 1 minute; stir until smooth after the first minute and continue to cook at 10- to 15-second intervals until there are no lumps.

Once the chocolate is melted, remove it from the heat source and add cherry juice.

Using your ⅜-ounce ice cream scoop, scoop out dough and place on parchment-lined cookie sheets 1 inch apart.

With your thumb, press in the center of each cookie to make a small well. Spoon ½ teaspoon chocolate sauce in middle of each cookie.

Bake 20 minutes, until bottoms are lightly browned and cookies are firm. Immediately after removing from the oven, work quickly to place one maraschino cherry on top of each chocolate center, pressing down lightly.

Let cool.

Drizzle cookies with remaining chocolate sauce and allow the chocolate to set before storing in an airtight container.

Makes approximately 44 cookies.

CHAPTER 3

AUNT NINA'S COOKBOOK

When I said that I wasn't sentimental about things, I wasn't being completely honest. I took one thing with me to Chicago that I was really attached to and that I still treasure to this day. In fact, if anything ever happened to it, I don't know what I'd do. It's my aunt Nina's cookbook.

Aunt Nina is the woman responsible for my love of cooking—and my love of cookies. But before I get into that, first you need some background.

Food wasn't something we thought a lot about in my household growing up, and in that regard we were no different from a lot of our neighbors. This was the '70s, era of those awesome TV dinners where everything was supposed to cook at exactly the same rate and temperature but nothing ever did. They never tasted as good as they looked on the box, but even still, we loved them. I mean, how cool was it to have your corn and your turkey in gravy and your apple pie all on the same aluminum dish in their own little slots? I also remember eating a lot of bologna in those days. I joke that I'm well preserved to this day from all the nitrates I consumed back then.

My mother made us dinner every night, even though cooking really wasn't her favorite thing to do. And none of us helped her in the kitchen either—certainly not my father, macho former marine. He wouldn't even help with the dishes. That was for girls (is it any wonder I hate to do dishes to this day?). But even though my mother didn't particularly enjoy cooking, she served us the same square meals all the other mothers in the neighborhood did—beef stew, broiled chicken, hamburgers, fish sticks. On Sundays we went to the local Chinese restaurant like every other Jewish family. Those are probably some of the happiest times we had together as a family. I remember it was old-school Cantonese—drinks served in tiki glasses with little umbrellas, fortune cookies, and chow mein—always chow mein.

Mostly though, food wasn't particularly special to me. It was just food.

Then we'd go to my aunt Nina's house, and all that would change. She was my father's sister-in-law. She and my uncle lived near my father's parents outside of Boston, and we'd visit them a few times a year.

I have such a potent memory of arriving at their door for visits. No matter the season, we'd walk in to smell something amazing. Her cranberry onion brisket was to die for—whenever I make it now, people lick their bowls. The same thing goes for her lemon herb chicken and her baked ziti. I loved it all.

One of the things that still amazes me about my aunt Nina was that her timing was always impeccable, which is the true sign of a great cook. No matter how many dishes she was making, they were all done at the right time and served at the right temperature. I still don't know how she did it. As much as I love to cook, the timing part of it makes me anxious. That's probably why I'm more of a baker—you don't have to serve cookies to temperature and you can make them in advance. There's no last-minute sweating and straining in the kitchen. But Aunt Nina never seemed to sweat, and she was so relaxed and happy in there that I'd even offer to help her with the dishes, which is something I'd never do at home.

Nina and my uncle had three kids close in age to me and my sisters, and it was hard not to notice how different their household was from ours. Aside from what Nina whipped up in their kitchen, their house was just calmer all around than ours was. Their town was a little closer to being rural than I was used to, and I remember being there in the winter and my cousins suggesting that we all go skating on the nearby pond. Skating on a *pond*? I couldn't wrap my brain around it.

It was so Norman Rockwell. Way more important, Nina and my uncle loved each other, and it showed. Their kids must have picked up a few pointers, too, because they've all been happily married for decades.

But back to the food. Nina was the one who made me realize that food could be wonderful, and it could also make you feel wonderful. Her recipes all came from her synagogue's cookbook that she and the other women had compiled as a fund-raising venture. I remember that the recipe pages she loved and used most were also the most food stained (the same way mine are now). And I remember my excitement when we first arrived for a visit, and I couldn't wait to find out what she was making. Out of that book came a seemingly endless series of delicious dishes—I especially loved a vanilla confection called blintz soufflé, not to mention beef Wellington (wrapped in crescent rolls, of course—everything's better wrapped in a crescent roll).

My aunt knew that I was her biggest admirer, so when she found out that I was moving out on my own she had a little gift for me—my own copy of her synagogue's cookbook. Now that's love. And that's one possession that I will never, ever give up. That's love, too.

This was the first "Jewish" dessert recipe I ever attempted. I can't remember a single holiday growing up when there wasn't a plate of these somewhere in the house. I've updated them a bit with the addition of toffee pieces. They're optional, but whether you were bat mitzvahed or not you should really give them a try because they make the recipe much more delicious. These cookies really are a taste and texture explosion in your mouth—they have a thin, crunchy outside layer, then they're sweet and chewy on the inside, with the added yum of the bits of chocolate and toffee. One boyfriend actually told me that they were like sex on his tongue. (If my aunt Nina's synagogue sisters only knew.) This is one powerful cookie. One final encouragement: this recipe is so easy and never-fail that if you're Jewish and you can't make it, then you might want to think about converting.

MERINGUE KISSES

2 egg whites	½ cup mini chocolate chips
1 teaspoon vanilla	¼ cup crushed toffee pieces
¾ cup granulated sugar	Parchment-lined cookie sheets

Preheat oven to 300 degrees.

Beat egg whites until they form soft peaks. Slowly add vanilla and sugar so as not to deflate the whites, then beat until stiff.

Fold in chips and toffee pieces.

Drop onto the cookie sheets in teaspoon-sized dollops about 2 inches apart. Bake about 25 minutes. You'll know they're done when they've puffed up a little bit and they're no longer shiny.

Cool completely and store in an airtight container.

Makes about 22 cookies.

CHAPTER 4

ON-AIR

When I left Long Island for Chicago, I had a couple of clear goals in mind:

1. Find my on-air voice.
2. Locate a boyfriend before it snowed.

I was starting my first big radio job, so you'd think goal number one would be foremost on my mind. But in some ways I figured goal number two was more urgent. I'd been warned about the cold. (It's the cliché of living in Chicago. Someone hears that you're moving there and what's the first thing they say? "Cold winters!") I'd also been warned about the snow, and I thought I'd better find a casual boyfriend before all the eligible men were buried under drifts.

The *casual* part of the boyfriend equation was key. I wasn't looking to fall in love, I just wanted a little romance. And as great and exciting a city as Chicago is, that was the same attitude I had toward it as a place to live. I wasn't aiming for marriage—my one true love (New York radio) was still waiting for me back home. Chicago would be a lovely interlude, a huge learning experience, and my first real job as an on-air personality. But it wasn't destined to be a forever kind of love.

Although I didn't hesitate for a second when the program director offered me the job, it wasn't an easy decision to make. On the one hand, I knew it was the right thing to do. On the other hand, I was genuinely terrified. As I prepared to leave home, I would be smacked with sudden, stomach-gripping bouts of panic and think, *Oh my God, what am I doing?* But I knew that if I wanted to end up on-air in New York, I needed to get some real major-market experience under my belt. So I packed my suitcase and I went.

This was back in the days long, long before Craigslist, so it wasn't as if I could find an apartment before I arrived. I couldn't google "where do nice single girls live in Chicago?" I flew into town on a Friday, knowing less than nothing, and I picked up a copy of the *Chicago Reader*. I ran my finger down the apartment listings and that very weekend I found myself a furnished alcove studio apartment with a view of Lake Michigan and wall-to-wall shag carpeting. Hadn't I told Barry that I'd have shag carpeting when I made it to the big time? And here I was.

I still remember the sight of the sun rising over the water—and the sound of the wind rattling against the windows. I could stand next to my bed and watch storms rise over the lake and slowly engulf the city. My first storm there was magical and frightening all at once—I couldn't believe how *loud* it was. I actually called a friend and held the receiver out the window so she could hear. Probably my fondest memories of Chicago revolve around that lake. It had its own climate and personality, and I loved the way Chicagoans spent so much of their lives on the beach—Rollerblading, biking, and festivals every summer weekend. In the summer Chicagoans didn't leave town on the weekends the way New Yorkers often do. They went to the lake.

That first night in my new apartment, I unpacked my clothes, and I shoved my one box of possessions into a closet. I never did unpack that box—it stayed right there until I moved back to New York a year and a half later. And three days after I arrived, I started my new job as the afternoon newsperson at WMET. I was all alone, just twenty-three years old, but the second I walked through those doors, the staff at WMET became my second family. There was such a sense of camaraderie. Everyone was young and ambitious, and we were all there for the same purpose. I've always found radio people welcoming,

but the people at WMET were especially friendly.
I don't know if was their midwestern charm, or if
it was some instinctive urge on their part to huddle
together against the approaching winter. Either way,
they accepted me with open arms.

I decided to return the favor by making sure I
didn't sound like an idiot out-of-towner. I studied
the map of Chicago like my life depended on it. I
learned how to pronounce Goethe Street correctly. I
memorized landmarks. I never—not once—referred
to Soldier Field as Soldier's Field, which any Chica-
goan will tell you is an offense worse than putting
catsup on a brat. I even learned to say gym shoes
instead of sneakers, and pop instead of soda. Before
long, I sounded like a local, which is the sign of a true
radio personality. We're all a bunch of chameleons.
And of course that kind of flexibility is also the foremost trait of a middle child like me—if you're going
to survive, you've got to adapt. I could always adapt
to a fault.

WMET was the new kid on the block in Chicago
rock radio. There was a progressive station that had
its little niche, and then there was our biggest competition, the Goliath to our David—WLUP, a.k.a.
"the Loop." They had a massive marketing budget
and billboards all over town. They could even afford
TV ads with a sexy blond babe in a tight T-shirt that
said THE LOOP in script right across her boobs. That
blonde had nothing whatsoever to do with the sta-

tion, but she looked hot (and totally braless) in the T-shirt. In one of the ads, the camera focused in tight on just her red-glossed lips while she lip-synched to the camera. Another ad ended with her spinning in front of the camera, and when she stopped she said, "Rock on, Chicago . . . *Pow.*" Then she made a finger gun that she shot at the viewer, pointed up at her lips, and slowly, insinuatingly blew on. They might as well have run the tagline, "Listen to the Loop and think about this woman having sex with you."

Meanwhile, I was trying to master talking like a local, while also sounding completely at ease on-air, as if the DJ and I had known each other for years and we were just hanging out over a couple of beers. Our time on-air was about being fun, easy, and light. Listeners were supposed to want to be friends with us—to think that we really would be their friends if we ever found ourselves in the same room together. And I was really, really good at that. This was when I learned something important about myself: I came alive at the microphone. I never thought anyone would look twice at me if they walked past me on the street. I didn't walk into a party and expect all eyes to look my way. I never felt pretty. But when I got behind the microphone and put on my headphones, all my self-consciousness fell away. Sure, thousands of people were listening to me, but I didn't worry about making a mistake or saying anything wrong. I was fearless. I had no problem teasing the

DJ, cracking jokes, and taking chances. We'd banter about the city, and what was happening in popular culture and the news. Basically, I got paid for what most people do at cocktail parties for free.

Of course that was just a version of me—the on-air version. I could pretend that I was revealing the real me, but I was protected by that microphone. The relationship between me and the listeners was simultaneously close and distant, just the perfect thing for a girl with a whole host of intimacy issues that she didn't even know about yet. I've always said that radio is where you can forget who you are or who you're supposed to be in real life, and you can just enjoy the moment. Behind that microphone was the only place I felt like that. To this day, being on the radio quiets all the other noise in my head. When the on-air light goes on, suddenly I'm in the moment in a way that's really hard for me otherwise. Some people need a cocktail to slow down—I just need a microphone and a set of headphones. It's no wonder my headphones became my constant companion over the years—wherever I went, they went. Some people pack up photos and tchotchkes when they change jobs or move offices—I just grab my headphones and I'm ready.

In a weird way it helped that WMET was the number two station in town. It gave me a public persona, but I didn't feel like a celebrity by any stretch. And we didn't feel insane pressure to be number one, which is something I can only really appreciate now. It was a different era, when a new radio format was given a little time to find its audience. That would never happen now. Radio stations come and go in less than a year if they don't make their mark, and everyone in the media feels a constant panic to survive. People are hired and fired in what seems like a heartbeat (just ask Ann Curry). It's crazy. Back then, we had a little room to breathe.

In time, little Lisa Glasberg became incredibly self-possessed behind the microphone, and I let my ambition drive me outside the studio too. When the Rolling Stones came to town, I decided that was my chance to scoop the Loop. As the number one station in town, staff there had all the advantages— exclusive ticket giveaways and much better positioning for broadcasting their show outside the stadium the night of the concert. We had none of that. So any little tidbit that I could find out about the band—any tiny factoid that the Loop didn't have—would be a huge coup. This was in the days before TMZ—there were no gossips going through celebrities' trash and tracking their every footstep the way they do now. So when I decided to sneak into the Stones' hotel and find out what they ordered from room service, it was considered a pretty big deal. People really wanted to know what Mick Jagger ate for breakfast, and I delivered, even if it meant sneaking onto their floor and digging through discarded trays of food scraps.

Then I decided to push the envelope even further, and I snuck onto their stage, which was supposed to be on total top-secret lockdown before the show. Mick's bacon and eggs turned out to be more exciting news, though. After all the hoops I had to climb through to get onto that stage to see their set design, all I found there was an empty stage and a cleaning lady with a mop and a bucket of Spic and Span. While I was standing there shaking my head at the totally anticlimactic scene, two security guards for the Stones discovered me. They each put a hand under one of my armpits and carried me off the stage and gently dumped me into the cinder-block hall.

Not long after, the newsperson for the morning show was sick and the general manager asked me if I'd ever done morning radio before. I said I hadn't, and he said, "Well, now you are." This was a huge break for me. The morning shift was way more prestigious than the afternoon, because that's when there was a larger audience and therefore bigger ad dollars that made more money for the station. I should have been intimidated at the prospect, but I remember feeling completely at ease. The DJ for the morning shift was a lovely guy named John Fisher, and he and I hit it off immediately. We were both silly and funny, and the general manager must have liked our rapport, because the next day he asked me to take the job permanently. I jumped at the chance. Morning radio was the big time.

Things continued to go well, and the radio station higher-ups finally decided that they would spring for one big billboard ad for our morning show. Our competitor had that sexy blonde in its ads, but I guess WMET couldn't afford a photo shoot, so our billboard just featured the station's blue-and-yellow logo. And the only location they could swing was way out on the expressway that led to O'Hare airport. Then they got the bright idea that it would be fun if we did our show live by remote, in front of the billboard. Bear in mind that this ad was on the top of a building, and we were doing a morning show. Even in the summer you could freeze your butt off at 6 A.M., so they practically had to chain us to that rooftop to keep us from being carried off by a strong gust of wind. It was like an episode right out of that old sitcom *WKRP in Cincinnati*. Did the station really think we were going to get one more listener by broadcasting in the middle of nowhere? Who had the time to look up at us while they were rushing to or from O'Hare airport? And where was my sexy T-shirt and finger gun?

Meanwhile, my days of normal working hours were over for good, and I didn't know what hit me. My very civilized noon-to-seven shift was a thing of the past and now I was getting up at 4 A.M., walking to the station in the dark, finding the one open place to get my coffee and doughnut on the way. Sometimes I was convinced a strong wind would not just bowl me over, but blow me away. The last anyone would see of me would be a blip on the horizon above Lake Michigan. I seriously considered putting weights in my shoes.

Soon after I started the new shift, a friend of mine from New York visited, and of course he wanted to go out in the evenings. I dutifully went along, and it was like the most extreme form of torture just to hold my eyes open. I felt physically ill. All I wanted to do—for the rest of my life—was sleep. Deep down in my bones I craved a nap.

I had officially become a sleep junkie, as all morning radio people are. We're forever looking to catch up somewhere, anywhere, as if an extra hour of sleep here or a quick snooze there will finally satisfy us. But the truth is that we'll never be satisfied, we'll always crave that next bump. Around this time I caught a look at myself in the mirror and I saw a stranger staring back at me with massive, unfamiliar bags under her eyes. I remember thinking, *Oh, I do not know if I am cut out for looking old before my time.* But that's the trade-off—if it was a choice between morning radio and my looks, then morning radio would win every time. So I got used to being tired.

I also got used to goose down. My big investment of the new job was to buy myself a Michelin-man-sized hooded down coat that went all the way to the ground. Sexy it was not, but warm it was. Luckily, I'd already found a boyfriend by then. Scratch off goal number two. Time to make a new list.

What better confection to symbolize the climate of my new (albeit temporary) home than snowballs? The chocolate batter means that the snow looks more like a dusting once they're baked, but I guarantee that no one you serve them to will complain.

CHOCOLATE SNOWBALLS

½ cup all-purpose flour
½ cup sugar
¼ cup unsweetened Dutch-
   process cocoa
½ teaspoon baking powder

2 tablespoons unsalted butter, at
   room temperature
1 large egg
Parchment-lined cookie sheets

For coating the snowballs, in separate small bowls
½ cup granulated sugar

½ cup confectioners' sugar

Preheat oven to 400 degrees.

In a metal or freezer-safe bowl mix flour, sugar, cocoa, and baking powder. One at a time mix in butter and egg until well blended. Chill in the freezer for 10 minutes, or until the batter is firm.

Using a small ice cream scoop, scoop out dough, and use your hands to roll each scoop into a ball. Then roll each ball in granulated sugar first, followed by confectioners' sugar, until completely coated.

Place balls on cookie sheets about 1½ inches apart. Be careful when loading your filled trays into the oven, so your little dough balls don't decide to roll off and make a break for it.

Bake 8 to 10 minutes, until cookies are set (they will appear crackled on the outside).

Cool on racks.

Makes 24 cookies.

CHAPTER 5

MARRIED AND UNAVAILABLE

When you play a part for a living, it can be hard for people to figure out where you end and where your public persona begins. Truthfully, for many years after I first started in radio, I often didn't know where the dividing line was myself. I carried my on-air personality around with me like a candy coating. Was I the happy-go-lucky girl I played on the radio, or was I someone else? Did it really matter? After all, I could be whoever I needed to be.

Just recently I found an old promotional interview WMET did for all its radio personalities, and I had to laugh at mine.

Born to Run may actually have been my favorite album at the time, but there's no way my fantasy was "to fall in love and hear bells." It was a good sound bite, though, so that's what I said to the interviewer.

LISA GLASBERG

Favorite album: Springsteen "Born to Run"
What's the best concert you've ever seen in Chicago? Why?: Springsteen—Uptown, October, 1980. Felt like I jogged 10 miles when it was over.
What is your favorite Chicago concert hall? Why?: Auditorium Theatre—enjoy the acoustics.
Goal: To read marijuana futures right along with pork bellies on WMET's Hog Report.
Favorite sport: To watch the Chicago Bears in the locker room.
Fantasy: To fall in love and hear bells (not from the AP wire machine).

To me it didn't even feel like a lie. I was just being entertaining, which is what everyone wanted from me—and what I wanted from myself. If I'd been answering truthfully, though, I would have said that my job was the only long-term relationship I was looking for.

It's a good thing that marriage and children weren't even slightly on my mind at that point in life, because a career in radio is not conducive to settling down. The hours were just one downside—even men who thought they could be flexible eventually got tired of dating someone who needed to be in bed by nine. But even more challenging than the schedule was the all-consuming nature of being on the radio. Compared to the thrill of my work life, a quiet dinner and a movie with a nine-to-five kind of guy seemed . . . boring. My work was a constant buzz, and it was hard to come down from that into the reality of the day to day. I had a really hard time faking interest in a boyfriend's ups and downs at the office while I was hanging out with rock stars. ("Really, honey? Tell me more about that memo you wrote.") At that point in life, my sole focus was on myself and my career. And that became a habit it would take a very long time to break.

I'm sure a lot of twentysomethings go through this to one degree or another. This is the decade when you're building your career and it's considered acceptable to be a little selfish about it. Working long hours and being ambitious is admirable. But still, I think most people at this age are also starting to try to narrow in on a potential partner, and to figure out how to strike a balance between work and personal life. That urge never clicked in for me, though, and I never had the slightest pang of jealousy when other girls talked about their boyfriends or mooned over engagement rings. That was not my thing. Work was my thing.

Strangely enough, as important as my job was to me, I had a real insecurity about guys only liking me for what I did for a living. When I met men outside of the radio business, I'd often lie to them about my work, at least at first, because I wanted them to be interested in me, not my call letters. When I did finally tell them that I worked at a radio station, they loved it. What wasn't to love? The parties I got them invited to were awesome, and the people I introduced them to were cool and interesting. If guys could put up with my insane schedule, then I was pretty fun to go out with. But did they like me for *me*? I didn't think so.

Maybe that's why I was more comfortable around people in the business. With the exception of my sweet upstairs neighbor, my social life revolved around work. I made friends with the woman who owned the restaurant downstairs from the station. I played on the WMET softball team. I went to all the promotional parties. Work was my social life, and my social life was my work. So it only made sense that I met my first Chicago boyfriend while I was covering a story. We were at a news conference at Navy Pier, and I was waiting around with all the other pool reporters when Rick walked right up to me. "You're new in town, aren't you," he said.

Rick was a television sports reporter—tall, WASPy, and the dictionary definition of handsome. He always wore a blazer, corduroy pants, and loafers, and his hair was neatly side parted. He was like a living Ken doll. I knew that I was no Barbie, so when he first started flirting with me, I kind of looked to my right and my left to see what cute girl he was talking to. It couldn't possibly be me. I was so insecure about my looks that it never occurred to me that I could be the target of his interest. But I managed to smile and even flirt back a little bit.

I said, "Well, I guess you can tell as soon as I open my mouth that I'm not from around here. But don't let my New York accent scare you." Then I immediately wondered why I'd said that to this nice midwestern boy. He'd surely walk away in horror.

To my surprise and relief, he laughed. "Are you kidding me? I deal with Chicago aldermen. Nothing scares me anymore."

The local TV reporters were like gods in Chicago, so Rick was a true celebrity in town. I was only the unknown newsperson for the distantly second-rated rock radio station. Rick and I didn't just travel in different circles, we were from different solar systems. When he asked me to go out with him and the other TV people, it was like being invited to hang out with the popular kids in high school. I didn't kid myself that I was one of them, but I enjoyed the borrowed glow.

This was when I learned how to like beer and talk sports. The first time I was at an upscale bar on Rush Street with Rick and his friends (who all looked like well-groomed fraternity boys but who were also genuinely nice), Rick asked me what I wanted to drink.

I looked around at what everyone else was drinking, and I said, "I guess I'll have a beer."

Rick laughed and said, "What kind of beer? They've got five different kinds on tap." This was news to me, because at the bars I went to back in New York, a beer meant a Bud, plain and simple. So that's what I settled on, and then I tried to blend in with the conversation, which always seemed to be about one of two topics: (1) work at the TV station, which I could handle, because all my radio friends and I talked about was work, too, and (2) the Bears. I had to brush up on my football knowledge mighty quick if I was going to hold my own with these guys. It was a good thing that Gary Fencik of the Bears was a good friend of the radio station's staff, so I could drop his name and sound like I knew him—and also come across as if I knew what I was talking about.

Rick and I might not have been the most natural fit, but amazingly (to me), he seemed to genuinely like me, and soon he was zipping me around town in his car, taking me shopping for sweaters out in the suburbs where all the other WASPs gathered. This was completely unfamiliar terrain for me. Half my wardrobe was made up of promotional T-shirts, and the other half was denim. If I was going to date Rick, I knew I had to step up my game clothing-wise. Overalls and rock concert T-shirts were not going to cut it in his crowd. So on my next trip home to New York I went shopping. And there, in the Norma Kamali store, I found the Magic Purple Jumpsuit.

It fit me like a second skin, and it showed more of my 32C cleavage than anyone even knew I had. The impact it had in my little world in Chicago was as dramatic as that famous green-print Versace dress that J.Lo wore to the Grammys. My purple jumpsuit was *life changing*. Suddenly, I felt feminine, and I loved it. I also loved the effect it had on Rick and every other guy who saw me in it. If I made one wrong (or right) move, the goods would be fully on display, and I could see the expectant look on their faces. It was the first time in my life when I experienced the power of attracting men physically. And I used that power for good and evil. Poor Rick never had a chance.

Our evenings together inevitably went something like this: He'd take me out to dinner somewhere nice. After dinner, on our way out of the restaurant, we'd be chatting and laughing and it seemed only natural to suggest getting a drink somewhere to keep the good mood going. Then, by the time we left the bar, I would look at my watch in pretend surprise and say, "Oh my God, I didn't realize it was so late! I have to be up in the morning!"

That was always the perfect excuse, and it worked every time. It had the benefit of being true, and any guy who wasn't a jerk couldn't argue with the fact that I had to be awake and on-air when he could still be fast asleep in his bed. As Rick and I got more serious, he got a little more persistent, and I'd let him come up to my apartment. But I'd always say, "Just for a few minutes, because I have to be up in the morning."

In my apartment, we'd make out a bit, and I'd let him get to second or third base, but that was it. Then I'd call time-out and send him home with a good-night kiss and a thanks for the memories.

Rick was looking for a girlfriend, but I didn't

know the first thing about how to be a good one. I had a great time with him, but dressing up for him was as far as I would take things emotionally. He might as well have been dating my jumpsuit for all he got out of me. It was crazy, really. Here was a gorgeous, successful man who seemed nuts about me, and yet I wouldn't even sleep with him. It wasn't prudishness that was stopping me—I was as ready as the next girl to jump into bed. But Rick was the real thing. He was the kind of guy you could fall in love with. The kind of guy you could marry. And that stamped a big X on his forehead as far as I was concerned.

So instead of settling down with Rick, I found myself drawn to Bryan, who was like Rick's evil twin.

Bryan was one of the record promoters who came every Tuesday to meet with our music director and convince him to play their songs. These guys weren't like the goofy-looking studio staff I was used to. They were smooth. All these suave, well-dressed men would wait patiently in the lobby for their names to be called. One by one, they'd parade by the newsroom window, cool leather briefcases in hand, hoping their songs would make our playlists—giving me ample time to flirt with them.

I thought Bryan was incredibly good-looking. He was six foot three and slim, with long blond hair, perfect features, and bedroom eyes. And he always made a point of stopping by my desk to chat.

He had a kind of electricity around him, very different from what I felt with Joe. So I asked one of the other women at the station about him. "What's his story?" I said to her.

"Him?" she said, giving Bryan a knowing look. "That one's off-limits. Very married. And she's hot, so don't even bother trying."

"Well, that hasn't stopped me before," I said. She raised her eyebrows at me, and I smiled like I had all the confidence in the world. In truth, I had no self-esteem whatsoever or I wouldn't even have thought of going after a married man. But I figured he was giving me plenty of signals that he was interested in me, so this was a perfect challenge for me—a way of proving to myself that I mattered, that I was noticeable. That familiar old ticker tape ran through my head, *News flash, Lisa, if this guy chooses to be with you instead of his wife, then you're really worth something!*

I fell hard for Bryan. We moved our flirting in the office to flirting in bars and promotional showcases, and it got to the point where we were talking to each other more than anyone else, holding our heads too close, everything short of touching. Finally, when the suspense was beyond killing me, he leaned into me and said these immortal words, "Things aren't good with my wife. We're kind of doing our own thing right now. I'm not really sure what's going to happen with us."

I should have heard brakes screeching to a halt, but instead I heard violins. Music to my ears. If things weren't good with his wife, then things might be better with me, right? And that made it okay, right? To be honest, if he'd confessed to me that he had his wife locked up in his basement, I probably still would have been into him. But thankfully he made it sound like he and his wife were on the verge of breaking up, which was perfect for easing my conscience. In my lust-addled brain that translated to, "Yay! Let's have sex!"

As slow as I'd been with Rick, I threw caution to the wind with Bryan. The first time I brought him back to my little studio apartment, I couldn't tear off my purple jumpsuit fast enough. We started making out at the entrance to my building and had shed several layers of clothing by the time we got to my door, ignoring my gawking neighbors along the way. I remember feeling absolutely giddy with the sexual thrill of being with him. I could have bottled that sensation and sold it as Viagra, it was just that powerful. It was pure, unadulterated youthful lust, that rush of feeling like every cell in your body is alive and crying out for the same thing. This was the way passion was supposed to be (I thought). Like forbidden love in a movie. Like that scene in *Fatal Attraction* when Michael Douglas and Glenn Close go at it in the elevator—before things take a turn for the worse.

Bryan was so tall that his legs hung out over the edge of my twin bed, and it was a gymnastic event just getting undressed the rest of the way. It was like having sex on a balance beam. I'm sure I said, "Ouch, my hair," every time he leaned the wrong way, but instead of dampening our desire it just ratcheted it up. What we lacked in grace we made up for in enthusiasm. This was the first time in my life that I was ever totally, completely sexually hung up on a man. Everything before this had been child's play. Bryan was no child.

Afterward, my apartment looked like a hurricane had swept through—bra, shoes, coats, pants strewn everywhere, books and dishes knocked off tables. Outside, though, the weather was beautifully calm. I watched the snow falling on the other side of my window, and everything seemed so perfect and cozy right where I was. I had a gorgeous man in my bed, so who cared if winter was upon us? My mission was accomplished.

Irony of ironies, Bryan was as unavailable as Rick was available, and what was my response? I was crazy for him. I remember when he got up to go home to his wife a few hours later, I reached out to him and said, "Can't you stay longer?"

"Gotta get back. A late night is one thing, all night is something else," he said, pulling on his pants.

Right then I should have said, "But I thought you guys were doing your own thing?" I should have asked what he was doing with me instead of his wife. But I didn't ask, because I didn't want to know the answer.

I wish I could go back in time, shake my younger self, and say, "What are you doing? Tell him to go away and call you when he's divorced!" But no one— not even future me—could have sat me down and talked sense into me. I was hypnotized. The ticker tape just kept running through my head: *He wants to be with me! This is great!*

It would take years of spinning my wheels and putting energy into the wrong things before I learned how to be true to myself and what I deserved. So I kept repeating this pattern of wasting my time and emotionally investing in the wrong men. Instead of building something real that I could nurture and grow and call my own—and with someone who was open and available—I contented myself with the thrill of forbidden sex. Maybe that's why I'm not a judgmental person to this day. Having made so many mistakes myself, who am I to look down on other young women who don't realize that they have more to offer than a great ass?

All the while I was getting in deeper with Bryan, I stopped answering Rick's calls. It didn't take long for him to get the message. Years later, I wasn't at all surprised to hear that Rick had married and had five kids. Like I said, he was the settling-down kind. And supposedly, I wasn't. And it's true that I never expected Bryan to leave his wife—I certainly never asked him to. I didn't plan my personal life more than a day in advance—it was my career that I fantasized about, not a white wedding. But for all my insistence that I was just biding my time until New York radio called again, if Bryan had broken up with his wife and asked me to stay in Chicago, I would have. I was just that addicted to him, and my relationship antennae were just that twisted. I tossed aside a guy who would have wanted me to stay in Chicago, and I hopelessly trailed a guy who never would.

In my defense, I was tenderhearted putty in Bryan's experienced hands. He was a master at the infidelity game. He dangled me like a professional, drew me close when I might have wandered, but then when I seemed like I was a little too into him, he'd push me away again and remind me, "I'm still married, you know." And the kicker? When I made the mistake of referring to the two of us as a couple, he actually said to me, "You know, we're not really together." And no, I didn't slap him in the face in response.

Fool me once, shame on you. Fool me a hundred times or so, and I'll finally get with the program. Eventually I woke up from my stupor, and when New York did call—exactly one and a half years after I'd arrived in Chicago—I was ready to go home.

I was such a ding dong when it came to men at this point in my life, and no wonder. I didn't have brothers, and my father was such a formidable, unyielding presence in my life. I found men magnetic and incomprehensible all at once. Over the coming years, I would date man after man, a whole string of them, trying to figure out what made them tick, and which ones were the keepers. You can make your own mental count of boyfriends past while making these truly delicious gingerbread men. They're the perfect combination of crisp and chewy. You can even decorate them to resemble your exes, which can make it doubly satisfying when you bite their heads off. And if a leg or an arm falls off while you're transporting them to the baking sheets, no worries. They're just cookies.

GINGERBREAD MEN

3 cups all-purpose flour
¾ cup dark brown sugar
1 tablespoon cinnamon
1 tablespoon ground ginger
¾ teaspoon baking soda
1½ sticks unsalted butter, softened slightly
¾ cup robust molasses

2 tablespoons milk

5-inch gingerbread man cookie cutter
Rolling pin
Parchment paper for rolling and for lining cookie sheets

Using a standing mixer (preferable, since this is a heavy batter) or handheld electric mixer, blend all the dry ingredients. Add butter one tablespoon slice at a time, until butter is incorporated and dough resembles sand.

Add molasses and milk just until combined. Don't overmix.

Divide dough into three sections. Put each section between two pieces of parchment paper and roll ¼-inch thick. Stack sandwiched dough on a baking sheet and place in freezer until firm, about 15 to 20 minutes. Or you can refrigerate for 2 hours. Be patient at this stage; don't try to rush it. Trust me, you'll thank me later.

Meanwhile, preheat oven to 350 degrees.

Line cookie sheets with parchment paper. Remove one sheet of dough at a time. Make sure it is very firm—this is really important if you don't want to have a breakdown when you try to use the cookie cutter. Now cut out your man shapes and transfer them to the prepared baking sheet using a wide cookie spatula. Space them 1 inch apart. Set scraps aside.

Repeat with remaining sheets of dough. Gather scraps of dough, form a ball, and place between two pieces of parchment paper. Roll ¼-inch thick. Refreeze, and then repeat the rolling and cutting.

Bake cookies 10 to 12 minutes. Cookies should barely spring back when touched in center. The longer you cook the cookies, the crisper they will be. You have all the power in this relationship!

Makes around 21 five-inch gingerbread men.

CHAPTER 6

SLEEPLESS IN MANHATTAN

The call came from the ABC Radio Network, the largest syndicated radio network in the country. This was national radio out of New York, a world away from the local radio that I was used to. It was like I'd been called up to the majors.

Always ambitious, forever keeping my eyes on the prize, I had stayed in touch with all my old New York colleagues, one of whom was Walter Sabo, who worked in programming at the ABC Radio Network. At the time, they were starting a new rock radio network, and they needed a newsperson. I was the first person Walter thought of, and I barely let him get the job offer out of his mouth before I was jumping up and down in my Chicago studio apartment and screaming "yes." I think my bag was packed even before I hung up the phone.

John Fisher, my partner at WMET, was so disappointed when I told him I was leaving. He couldn't understand how I could give up the great thing we had going there. For him, Chicago radio was the Holy Grail. Other people at the station felt the same way— they'd say, "How can you leave? Chicago is such a great city." But my mind couldn't even compute that. Of course now I understand, but back then I was honestly shocked by their response. To me, it was all business. WMET wasn't home to me the way it was to them—it was a stepping-stone.

That was why I'd never settled in—or unpacked that box in my closet. That was why I'd let my relationship with Rick fade away. I didn't have time for getting attached—I had a dream waiting for me. The opportunity Walter offered me was irresistible. There was no thinking or debating to be done. I didn't look back, I didn't think twice. It's amazing how sure of myself I could be when it came to work. The downside, though, was that I don't think I ever really lived in the moment while I was in Chicago. I always had one foot out the door, one finger already turning the page. Next, next, next—that was how I lived my life.

Back in New York, I sublet a furnished apartment (I swear I didn't buy a stick of furniture until I was well into my twenties), and started work at the ABC Radio Network studio near Lincoln Center. In the 1980s, that neighborhood wasn't polished and accessible the way it is now. It was still basically Hell's Kitchen in those days, and not in a cool way. So it wasn't the nicest spot to work in, and it was particularly desolate during the wee hours of the morning when I'd be dragging myself into work.

My job title was News Anchor, Rock Radio Network, mornings. ABC consisted of multiple networks, and we had the entire floor of a city-block-sized building. It was one massive newsroom with frantically loud AP machines that dinged and danged every time an update or news bulletin came through. All the anchors sat at long tables, and desk assistants would come around every few minutes bringing us updates from the machines. They'd be printed out on long pieces of paper that spelled out all the top news events and sports. It was my job to weed through all that and cull it down to the short segments that I would read on-air. After a couple of hours of this endless stream of AP reports, my desk would look like the Alps if I wasn't careful, and my hands would be black from the ink of newspapers and printer carbon. I still remember the smell of that carbon, and how grimy and disgusting I'd feel by the end of the day. In its own way, it was just as unglamorous as my first local radio jobs.

I became rigorously tidy, because it was the only way to survive the onslaught. I would neatly stack all my stories in piles—local, national, features, and sports. I was hired to bring some sparkle to the news broadcasts, and to emphasize the entertainment reporting, and I learned from the much older anchors around me how to write economical copy while punching it up with my personality.

After typing up my newscast, I would walk down a long hallway to an airtight booth where it would be just me and a microphone on one side of a glass partition, and a sound engineer on the other. That was it—there was no lighthearted bantering with a DJ, no relaxed and easy conversation.

My time in that booth was incredibly lonely and high pressure. Because my broadcast was syndicated, which meant that all the rock stations that were part of the network would be picking it up, everything I said had to be timed to the second or I'd be cut off. This was a terrifying prospect. Other than dead air, there's nothing worse in radio than being cut off midsentence. So I learned not only to write the exact number of words that I needed, but also how to pace myself and deliver my broadcast in exactly three minutes. It was nerve-racking, and to this day if you told me to write three minutes of text, I could do it in my sleep.

My sound engineer didn't help my nerves. He was odd and unfriendly and single-mindedly focused on his job, which was to tell me when I was on and off the air. He looked like Poindexter from the old Felix the Cat cartoons, minus the mortarboard. He had the same black-framed Coke bottle glasses, and he had the strangest way of signaling to me. Instead of just pointing at me when I was on-air, he'd raise both his hands out in front of him and slowly bring his fingers together like he was shooting a gun at me. The moment the tips of his index fingers touched, that was my signal that I was on the air. It was the weirdest thing, and I felt on edge every second I spent in that booth staring at him. Whenever he brought his fingers together I literally jumped in my seat.

The upside of all that stress, though, was that I learned a ton and this truly was the big time. And for the first time in my life I was making real money. No longer did I have to count my pennies every month to make sure I could cover the rent. I remember my first big splurge was to buy myself an expensive suede jacket. That was huge for me—other than my magic purple jumpsuit, I didn't spend money on myself, and I felt really proud that I could take care of myself now. My whole childhood, I had been aware of the power of money, and I had always wanted to be independent, to never feel that I had to ask my parents for support in that way. And now, I knew I'd never have to.

I had been grateful for the distance that Chicago gave me from my family. The job at WMET came at a point when I needed to carve out my own identity, totally separate from how my immediate family viewed me. Another reason to want some space from them was that my parents were going through a pretty acrimonious divorce at the time, and I made a conscious decision not to be drawn into the middle.

Back in New York, I was physically close to my family again, but emotionally I felt just as far away from them as ever. I think a lot of parents have a hard time seeing their children as adults, and mine were no different. I felt that they wanted me to stay little Lisa Glasberg, the girl they last knew as a teenager. But I wasn't that girl anymore, and I didn't want to pretend to be.

Not long after I started at ABC, my older sister, Bonnie, got married. I was working hard, and I decided to buy myself a really nice dress for the occasion. It cost $300, which seemed absolutely exorbitant to me at the time, but also incredibly special. I remember feeling like my family judged me for spending so much money, like they thought it was reckless or inappropriate. Ultimately, what I think it came down to is that I was upsetting

the apple cart. I had grown up and become someone that they didn't really know anymore, and I'm
sure that was alarming for them. They'd gotten used
to things being a certain way, and suddenly I was
changing the rules on them. I'm sure if you asked
my parents or my sisters, they'd remember things
completely differently, but at the time, I didn't feel
that my family got me, or what I really wanted from
life. And I can't really blame them for that—I was
still trying to figure it out myself.

I MAY HAVE LEFT the impression in the last chapter
that I ended things with Bryan once and for all when
I left Chicago. So let me correct the record: I didn't.

My career would always be my first love, but
Bryan still had a powerful hold on me. In a warped
way, I was once again looking to a man to fill the
role of father figure for me—he was older and I let
him kind of take charge, and he was just as unavailable as my dad had ever been. You know what they
say—you keep repeating bad habits because they're
comfortable. When I moved back to New York, I
think I really did believe that it was over with Bryan,
but then I'd concoct reasons to go back to Chicago
for visits—ostensibly to see girlfriends, but really I
was always hoping to hook up with Bryan. Pretty
soon, he was dropping in on me in New York, too.
It went on that way for a couple years. He made me

laugh when we were together, and he'd call every now and then when we were apart—always giving me just enough to keep me hanging in there.

But why was I hanging in there? Where did I think this relationship was going? I wasn't asking myself any of those questions, and I wasn't asking Bryan, either. I definitely didn't ask him about his wife. It's ironic that my career was all about asking people questions and pressing them to reveal themselves to me, because I didn't press Bryan for anything, and I certainly wasn't revealing anything about myself. I would never have told him what I really wanted from our relationship. I couldn't even admit it to myself. I just ignored my feelings and pretended that they didn't exist. When I was a kid, I was convinced that my feelings didn't matter, and now that I was an adult, I was still telling myself that my feelings didn't matter.

I didn't really believe that Bryan would leave his wife for me. But if I'm truly honest, then on some level I must have held out the tiniest bit of hope. That's why I kept answering his calls and bending over backward for him whenever he had a few hours for me. I was addicted to the way it felt when he was with me. Any little grain of attention from him made me feel like a million dollars. And when I sensed him pulling away—when gradually his trips to New York were fewer and farther between, and when he came up with more excuses for why he couldn't see me—instead of having the self-respect to call it off myself, I was even more eager to drop everything to be with him.

Arlene, me, and a friend.

Bryan was bad for me in pretty much every way, but I will always be grateful that he introduced me to Arlene, who in turn introduced me to New York nightlife. I'd had plenty of fun in Chicago, but nothing like what Arlene and I got into in New York. Arlene and I are still fast friends, and she's just as gorgeous now as she was then. She's a tall, blond knockout, and I was petite and cute, and when we both got dressed up for a night out, doors would open and velvet ropes would part. She always wore pink frosted lipstick, and her favorite outfit consisted of a pink leather micro miniskirt with gold zippers on the sides, a tiny T-shirt, and pointy-toed spike heels. I had a black leather miniskirt that I wore all the time, but somehow my outfits never looked as pulled together as hers did. For me it was more like a costume, like I was playing dress-up, but she always wore her outfits like she owned them. We'd both get our hair cut and highlighted at La Coupe, a very ritzy salon uptown. I wore mine in a long English shag.

On a typical night out, I'd arrive at Arlene's small loft apartment in Greenwich Village around 10 P.M. We'd get loaded on Quaaludes and cocaine (Arlene's doorman was also her supplier), and then we'd head out to Carumba, a popular Mexican restaurant near her apartment. The food was secondary to the margaritas, which we'd pound back like they were soda. Some nights we'd go to Marylou's, a café in Greenwich Village where people would do lines of coke off their dinner plates. Or maybe we'd go to the Odeon in Tribeca, where all the MTV VJs hung out. Then we'd go dancing at Heartbreak, or we'd hit a record company party where there was always an open bar and free food. Or we'd catch some up-and-coming band at the Bottom Line and then go have burgers and fries at the old Silver Spurs Diner.

I would like to say that I did all my partying on the weekend when I didn't have to get up for work the next morning, but that wouldn't be strictly true. In fact it wouldn't be true at all. Routinely, I'd end up going back to Arlene's place after we'd hit every possible club or party. Sometimes I'd crash for a few hours; other times I'd be too wired to sleep. Then she'd have to literally prop me up to get me into a cab to take me to work. She told me recently that at least once I was still slurring when I headed off to work. On the nights when I made it back to my apartment, I'd go to bed in my makeup and lie flat on my back so that I wouldn't have to waste time reapplying the next morning. I was so exhausted all the time that once I remember I actually staggered out of bed in the morning and got into the shower with my sweat socks still on my feet.

Today this might sound horrifying, and if you know a twenty-five-year-old acting like this (we can all think of a few starlets who fit this description), you might want to stage an intervention. I look at pictures of these girls now, caught in paparazzi pictures while they stumble out of clubs looking like they need a shower and some detox, and I can only imagine what I looked like when I was partying all night. I was lucky I had a friend like Arlene who ran protective circles around me instead of snapping embarrassing pictures of me for Facebook. It certainly never occurred to me that I was out of control. I was young and invincible, and I thought what a million other girls would think in the same situation—*oh, don't worry about me, I can handle it.* Colleagues now who hear about my partying all night are amazed, because I have a reputation for being the consummate professional, and I never let anything get in the way of my sleep. Back then, though, I was so used to dancing back and forth between my two lives, changing costumes, juggling plates, always moving, that it didn't occur to me to stop to rest.

As crazy as my lifestyle was, this was the '80s, and I was just one of an army of girls my age rolling out of bed a few precious hours after we'd rolled in. We all just splashed some cold water on our faces and drank a lot of coffee, and then off we went again. It was fun and exciting, and I was young, and I remember that whole time in my life being a constant thrill. Record companies had unlimited budgets in those days, and there was a nonstop stream of parties to go to and rock clubs with amazing live band performances. Arlene and I would dance and pound back White Russians at the Mud Club or the Ritz. Sting and Steven Tyler would be hanging out in the VIP section, and there was a door to a back room where you could get high.

I wouldn't do coke during the week—I wasn't that crazy—but I definitely indulged on the weekends. To me, it was recreational, no different from having a drink, and since I was tired all the time, I thought it was great how it perked me up. Luckily, I never felt it had the best of me, and it was so plentiful that I never had to waste my own money on it. Truthfully, I probably wouldn't have done it if I'd had to pay for it, but it was always around for the taking. I remember that I did keep a secret little stash in the jewelry box that my grandmother Muzzy brought me back from Japan. If she had known, she would've been horrified.

While Arlene and I were swinging from the chandeliers, we were also dating up a storm. I was still seeing Bryan when he came to town, but I certainly wasn't exclusive—I wasn't so delusional as to think I had to be faithful to a married man. Meanwhile, I still wasn't looking for a boyfriend, I just wanted to have some fun. So Arlene and I purposely dated all the wrong guys. We didn't care if they were nice, or if they had steady jobs. And we didn't care if any of our dates ever called us again, because we always knew we had each other. We just wanted the guys we were seeing to be good-looking and fun. And there were plenty of guys around that fit that description. Finding a man was like dropping a fishing line in the Everglades, it was that easy. You didn't even really need a hook. Arlene was addicted to the musicians, and to this day we joke that she dated every rock and roller who never made it.

My taste in men was no better than Arlene's. In fact, it was so bad that even when I thought I was choosing well, I wasn't. I met a nice Jewish dentist named Mark at a friend's party one time, and we hooked up that night. He lived in Brooklyn, so that was a little outside my comfort zone (I was Miss Sophisticated from Long Island, after all), but I figured: a Jewish dentist . . . cha-ching! This might even be a boy I could take home to Mom. And just think of all the free tooth bleaching I could get.

He was really good-looking, and he seemed like a lot of fun, and that would have been enough for me even without the job description. So I took Mark back to my apartment and we started making out and stripping down. We were lying on my bed, facing each other on our sides, I had my eyes closed, and out of nowhere . . . *smack!* Dr. Mark had just spanked me on my butt. My eyes flew open and before I could say *what the hell was that?*, he did it again.

Then I did say, "What the hell was that?"

He looked at me like he couldn't imagine why I was so surprised—like he spanked girls every day and usually they loved it. I should have kicked him in the privates and then told him that I do that every day and usually guys love it. Instead, I said, "Look, my butt's a no-fly zone and I'm not into spanking." He kind of shrugged and then continued on with things. Meanwhile, I was wondering if I was in bed with the dentist from *Little Shop of Horrors*.

Mark wasn't even slightly embarrassed when I ran into him on the street a few weeks later.

"Lisa," he said. "Where've you been? I've been calling you."

I'd been hoping he'd walk right by out of sheer mortification, but no such luck. "Oh, you know, working hard," I said. "Those early mornings are a killer." Meanwhile I was so obviously lying, looking anywhere but at his face. *Thank you, early mornings,* I thought to myself once again, *you've always been the perfect excuse.*

But that excuse didn't work on Dr. Spanker. "Well, let's get together sometime," he said. "I get up early, too. We can make it an early night." The way he said "early night" and smiled with his glistening pearly whites made me think of whips and chains, not milk and cookies.

"That would be great," I said, looking at my watch. "I'll call you! Gotta run!"

As I dashed down the street, all I could think was that this guy needed to lay off the sweet air. I figured I'd dodged a bullet the last time I'd gone out with him, and I was lucky that Dr. Spanker hadn't turned out to be Dr. Serial Killer.

I could get philosophical about how all the running, running, running that I did in those days was very effective at quieting the noise in my head. I couldn't imagine sitting still for a quiet dinner with a friend or boyfriend sans coke and white Russians. It just seemed . . . boring. All that distraction definitely prevented me from dealing with certain issues, or being at all introspective. If I didn't stop, then I didn't have to ponder why I didn't think I was worth more than a series of bad dates and a string of guys who were wrong for me in so many ways. And I definitely didn't have to ask myself why I made myself so unavailable to the few guys who would have been good for me.

Instead, I figured that it was time to let loose and live a little. I was tired of being responsible all the time—I'd been on a career track for years already and my job was high pressured, and I had the additional burden of supporting myself completely in an industry that wasn't always predictable. So at night, I shed all that. I got dressed up, and I shook off all that responsibility—and I shut off my brain for a little while.

I'D BEEN AT ABC Radio Network for two years when the grind of that little booth and Poindexter shooting finger guns at me finally wore me down. My heart just wasn't in it anymore, and I think the powers that be knew it. I missed local radio. I missed feeling a connection to the listener. I missed the phones lighting up, and the fun of playing off another human being at the microphone. Millions of people across the country might be listening to me on ABC, but I had no way of knowing it, or feeling it. I started to feel like I was wearing golden handcuffs—the pay was great, and hundreds of people would have killed for my job, but I just didn't love it. And while I could live without love with a boyfriend, I couldn't live without it in my work.

The final straw came when Bryan was visiting me. We went out with Arlene for one of our marathon nights of getting high, hitting a restaurant, then a club, then an after party, then an after-after party. Then Bryan and I went back to my apartment and had sex.

I didn't even need cocaine when I was with Bryan—he was my cocaine, and definitely my addiction, and I felt the same kind of artificial mental and physical high when I was with him. So the whole time I was with him it didn't occur to me that I should get some shut-eye before I headed to work the next morning. Why sleep when I had Bryan with me? I knew he'd fly off when morning came, so I wanted the night to last—I wanted him to last. Bryan was like a never-ending arcade game for me—I kept putting more and more coins into him but never winning the prize. And the lack of reward just made me more determined to keep trying. Instead of walking away, I just kept digging up more coins to dump into him.

The sky was still black that morning when Bryan turned to me and said, "You have to get to work, and I have a plane to catch." I fixed my raccoon eyes and found some reasonably clean clothes, and then we hopped into a cab together. As we pulled up in front of the station he kissed me and then drove off to JFK. I was on a romantic high, and definitely not fully sober. So I didn't read anything into that kiss, and I refused to admit to myself that he was moving on. I shouldn't have been surprised when he stopped calling me after that, but I was, and I was deeply hurt.

But that kind of hurt wasn't on my mind when I staggered into work at 4 A.M. that morning. I remember walking onto our floor at ABC Radio Network and being stabbed in the eyes by the fake sunlight of the fluorescent lighting, and the news machines chugging away echoed the pounding headache that was starting to build behind my temples.

The desk assistant started piling up the reports next to me, and I did the best I could to cut and paste them into something brief and logical. Before I knew it, it was time for my broadcast and I had to grab my typewritten stack and run to the booth where Poindexter was waiting for me.

Every day my format was the same. I started with national news, then features, followed by a thirty-second commercial break, and then sports. My papers were always neatly stacked and ready to go, and today was no different. One by one I read all my stories. The clock kept ticking away, and as always I watched the second hand with a close eye while reading and knowing exactly how long I had to finish. But when we got to the commercial break, I had no papers left. My sports report wasn't there. As the seconds of the commercial break counted down, I broke into a cold, slick flop sweat. I had typed up the sports report, I knew I had, but it wasn't there. Nothing was computerized so it's not as if I could pull up my missing report with a few keystrokes. Meanwhile there wasn't an intercom or a phone or big red panic button to hit to signal that I was in dire straits and needed help. There was just me, the microphone, and Poindexter's fingers making their slow, painful finger gun right at me. And dead air was not an option.

So I winged it. I'd love to say that I remembered enough of what I'd written that I pulled it off brilliantly. But I didn't. I remembered nothing, and I wasn't enough of a sports fan to bluster my way through it. I still have the text of that awful, terrible sports report, and I include it here for your horrified amusement as well:

A very active night, last night, at our country's ballparks. It seemed like most teams, in all divisions, were up at bat. And why not, the weather cooperated across most of the country, especially with the heat wave in the North East.

Stadiums were packed last night as fans spent a nice evening outside cheering their teams, with lots of runs being scored.

The White Sox really knocked it out of the park, as did the Yankees.

Usually at this time of year, teams are in top focus, with the smell of the World Series in the air. Before you know it—it's pennant season.

Here are some of last night's scores.

7 to 4

3 to 6

12 to 1

8 nothing

3 to 6

and 8 to 4

It's going to be a great division battle as we get down to the wire.

And that's sports.

I'm Lisa Glasberg on the ABC Rock Radio Network.

Aside from the totally inane preamble, what really kills me is the way I listed off random scores, not attaching a single one to an actual game, or even to a baseball team. It was complete insanity. You know what though? I may not have known what the heck I was saying, but there wasn't a second of dead air. I hadn't slept in thirty-six hours, and I was out of my mind with terror, but I was a professional. I didn't leave Poindexter alone with his on-air button.

At 9 A.M. that morning, the station manager called me into his office, and I knew my days were numbered. He didn't fire me then and there, but when my contract was up I learned that it wasn't being renewed. It wouldn't be long before I found out that my relationship with Bryan wasn't being renewed either. Two big endings came together in one day. And both were for the best, even if I wasn't in quite the frame of mind in that moment to admit it to myself.

Did I sabotage my relationship with ABC? It's possible. I know it was only a matter of time before I quit or they realized I wasn't cut out for sitting alone in a booth. But it's still a mystery to me what happened to that sports report I typed up. Maybe Poindexter stole it. The larger, much more important question that I needed to answer was how to find some happiness in my personal life. That was a mystery that I really did need to solve.

Since my life during these years was truly unhinged, I knew I wanted a recipe that featured nuts in this chapter. And because there's no better pick-me-up than chocolate, packing those nuts into a fudgy brownie was a no-brainer.

Not only are these brownies delicious, but they also gave me strength on those early mornings after I'd been partying late into the night. Even better, making them is a pretty good workout. If you're feeling like you want to burn off some frustration (career, romantic, whatever's currently getting you down), try mixing the batter using both hands and a big wooden spoon. You'll feel better in no time. I also recommend taking out your aggression on the nuts while you chop them. The more frustrated you are, the more nuts you can add. You can even sprinkle another layer on top of the chocolate frosting.

LISA GOES NUTS BROWNIES

For the brownies

10 ounces semisweet chocolate chips

¾ cup (1½ sticks) unsalted butter, at room temperature

1½ cups sugar

1½ teaspoons vanilla extract

4 large eggs

1 cup all-purpose flour

1 cup salted roasted cashews (roughly chopped)

For the peanut butter frosting and chocolate ganache

1 cup smooth (not natural) peanut butter

½ cup (1 stick) unsalted butter, divided

¾ cup confectioners' sugar

1 tablespoon whole milk

1 teaspoon vanilla extract

¾ cup salted roasted peanuts (roughly chopped)

7 ounces semisweet chocolate chips

Preheat oven to 325 degrees.

TO MAKE THE BROWNIES:

Line a 9 x 13–inch baking pan with parchment paper, so it overhangs on the short ends.

Over very low heat, melt chocolate chips and butter in a heavy saucepan.

When smooth, remove from heat. Stir in sugar (slowly), then vanilla, then eggs one at a time. Mix well after each addition. Fold in flour, then cashews.

Spread in prepared pan. Bake 25 to 30 minutes until tester inserted in center comes out clean.

Cool on a rack.

TO MAKE THE PEANUT BUTTER FROSTING:

Use an electric mixer to beat peanut butter and ¼ cup of the butter until fluffy. Add confectioners' sugar, then milk and vanilla. Spread the frosting gently over brownies with spatula. Now sprinkle the chopped peanuts over the peanut butter frosting, until covered. Gently press peanuts into frosting.

TO MAKE THE CHOCOLATE GANACHE:

Use a heavy saucepan over very low heat to melt chocolate and ¼ cup butter until smooth. Alternatively, you can use a microwave—slice butter into small pieces and place it and the chocolate in a covered microwavable bowl. Microwave on high for 1 minute then stir. Continue to microwave in 10- to 15-second increments until smooth.

Carefully spread the chocolate ganache over the peanut butter frosting.

Chill until firm, then remove the brownies from the pan using the overhanging parchment paper. Cut into 16 squares, and store in an airtight container (preferably in the fridge).

Makes 16 one-and-a-half-inch squares.

CHAPTER 7

FAKE 'N' BAKE

After the pressure-cooker atmosphere of ABC Radio Network, I was very happy to freelance for a while. There was a lot of work in radio those days—people went on vacation or took leaves, and they needed someone experienced to fill in. I could adapt my newscasts to any format and demographic, from rock to country to talk radio.

With my job demanding less of my time and energy, suddenly I didn't feel like I had to let off quite so much steam outside of work. I got Bryan out of my system once and for all, and I started to date men who might actually be boyfriend material.

The one problem with this plan was that I still had no idea how to be a girlfriend. And by extension, that meant that I really didn't know how a boyfriend should act either. I figured that being with a man was about making him want to stick around. I didn't ask myself what I wanted—or deserved—in a boyfriend. This was just another arena where I felt like I needed to prove myself to someone else. My years of dating lots of men had given me some confidence once the clothes came off, but I still had no real self-esteem underneath. And one way I decided that I could make a man like me was to bake for him. Because what man could resist a naked woman bearing cookies?

David was tall and lanky and came from a large Jewish family on the West Coast. He worked in the clothing business, and he seemed like such a responsible adult to me. His apartment looked like a home—unlike my haphazardly furnished place, which was a collection of preowned stopgap pieces. He had curtains that coordinated with his carpeting, and a fluffy down comforter on his bed. He was a metrosexual before there was a word for it. For a girl like me who had no roots at all—who had purposely avoided putting any down—the fact that he had this lovely, comfortable home was really attractive. I also felt safe in his high-rise apartment building with a doorman. I had always felt like I had to look out for myself, but there I felt cocooned, and like there was someone else who was taking care of things for a little while. In some ways I think I was more attracted to David's apartment than I was to him.

Part of the problem was that I didn't really spark

to him intellectually. It's not as if I was looking for an Ivy Leaguer. But I've always been drawn to people who think fast and talk just as fast. And I was surrounded by those kinds of people at work—people who had interesting thoughts about music, politics, and popular culture. Meanwhile, David was in the schmatte business, and he wasn't really interested in the world outside. He was all about numbers and order sheets and how many dresses he sold to Macy's.

Given that, you would think that I'd realize after a few dates that this guy wasn't for me. But he was good-looking, and I really did love his apartment. I also liked his family a lot and admired the way they enjoyed spending time together. So even though I really wasn't all that into David, the ticker tape that ran through my head was, *Nice apartment, nice family, why not date him?* Instead of admitting to myself that I found him boring and not all that bright, and despite all the clues that we were not a match, I persisted.

One cold winter evening we were snuggled up in his apartment on the sofa. It was election season and I wanted to turn on the news. He switched the channel to *Wheel of Fortune. Okay,* I told myself, *I can do this.*

I remember watching Vanna White revealing letter after letter until the clue read as follows:

WHEN _T RA_NS _T PO_RS

While the contestant struggled to figure out the clue, I said, "Oh my God, it's so obvious what that is. What a moron."

David looked at me and said, "It's not that obvious."

I made the mistake of laughing, and I said, "You're joking, right? I mean it's obviously 'When it rains it pours.'" When I saw David's jaw tighten, I realized that he was really angry with me. The lesson of that situation, whether it was one that I wanted to follow or not, was: never rub it in your boyfriend's face that you're smarter than he is.

For a while I told myself that David and I were growing close, but in retrospect I realize that no matter how much time we were spending together, I was never really his girlfriend. And at a certain point he started pulling away. We'd make plans, and then at the last minute he'd be busy. We'd go out together and I'd sense his eyes drawn to other women. While I didn't find David all that interesting, other women found him fascinating. To them, a successful man was a real catch. And the more that other women looked at him—and he looked at them—the more territorial I felt. So instead of letting the relationship run its course and finding someone better to lavish with my affections, I clung to David all the harder. Clearly, I had learned absolutely nothing from my Rick/Bryan experience, and I was the same old Lisa I'd ever been when it came to men. The less available a man was to me, the more I just had to have him.

One weekend afternoon we went roller-skating (this was the '80s, remember), and I wore a dark pink version of my magic purple jumpsuit. As we circled the rink, I noticed that he kept looking at one woman in particular. She was the female version of him in more ways than one—tall and dark, and she worked in the garment industry too. Soon he wasn't just looking at her, he was also stopping to flirt with her—while I was standing right there. A saner woman would have called it off with him on the spot, but (1) I was never very good at confrontation, and (2) I was not a saner woman.

Instead, I made cookies. I went back to my tiny studio apartment with the galley kitchen that you could barely turn around in. There was maybe a square foot of counter space, but it did have a really cool rubber floor that absorbed the shock whenever you dropped anything. The downside was that when I spilled flour it looked like a crime scene. Anyway, I whipped up a batch of my How-to-Get-a-Man Chocolate Chip Cheesecake Squares, then I stripped naked and put on my fur coat. After I'd left Chicago, I'd sworn like Scarlett O'Hara that I would never be cold again, so that fur coat was my reward. I'd also bought myself a Louis Vuitton overnight bag, which seemed like the height of style and sophistication to me. Since I was naked under the coat, I tossed some clothes in my bag, and out I went, cheesecake bars in hand. As I went sashaying down the street in my high heels, I ran into a friend who said, "Where are you off to?" I remember smiling and saying, "To see my boyfriend!" Even at the time I knew I wasn't telling the truth, and I honestly don't know why I lied. I think on some level it made me feel more worthy if I could use the *B* word.

My baking for love may have been totally dysfunctional, but it had the intended effect, at least for one night. David's eyes were wandering at the roller rink, but when I knocked on his door, he only had eyes for me. And he appreciated the chocolate chip cheesecake squares, too. So of course we immediately had sex, which, truth be told, wasn't all that great. Half the time I was faking it with David, which I always found way too easy to pull off. A few moans here, a crescendo there, and David felt like a god, while I was as romantically (and sexually) unfulfilled as ever.

David continued to give me signals that he wasn't being exclusive, but I just wasn't picking up on them. I did notice how testy he got whenever I talked about relationship stuff, though. I made myself way too available to him in a lot of ways, and I was never clingy or pushy about a commitment. I definitely wasn't looking to get married. But one night when we were lying in bed I started talking in a theoretical way about marriage, and whether he saw himself married with kids one day. To me, it was a natural question to ask, and I didn't see any strings attached to his answer. But you'd think I tossed a pot of cold water on him—he practically recoiled. So I went to sleep angry, he went to sleep horrified, and our relationship didn't last too long after that—especially once I found out that he was seeing Miss Tall Brunette at the roller rink.

Moral of the story: My cheesecake bars might help get a man, but keeping him is a different story.

THE WHOLE SEXUAL SATISFACTION thing is kind of fascinating to me. Judging from popular culture now, you'd think women sit around talking about their orgasms all the time. I suspect that's an exaggeration, and I know my girlfriends and I definitely weren't talking about it when we were in our twenties. My friends now will say, "Oh my God, we were such sluts," so I know we were all having a lot of sex. But were we always enjoying it? I'm not so sure. And since I spent a number of years there using a diaphragm, I can honestly say that I don't know how anyone can have an orgasm wearing one of those.

When I first started having sex, I don't know that I even realized that I was faking it. I mean, no one ever told me what an orgasm was supposed to feel like. I certainly felt something—excited, turned on, all that—so was that an orgasm? How the heck would I have known? It wasn't until I was truly in love with a man that I had my first real orgasm. And then I remember thinking, *Oh, I get it now.* All those years before that point, I was way more focused on how the man was feeling and whether I was doing it for him than whether he was doing it for me. I might as well not have been there at all—I could have just been a reflection in a mirror.

For me, the thrill was the romantic chase. I knew I had a good body, and I loved being the prize at the end of the chase. After feeling unattractive for so many years, being physically admired was a huge turn-on for me. I loved the power that I felt in bed with a man—I knew what to do, and I definitely knew how to please him. But I should have been more focused on how to please myself. Well, live and learn.

AROUND THIS TIME A lot of people in my life were marrying, and some were even starting families. As uninterested in marriage as I was, it's still hard not to feel a little left out when everyone's pairing off. It didn't help that people would give me sad looks when they were telling me their happy news, as if I needed reassurance or comforting. I remember once a really good friend of mine invited a bunch of us over to her new house to tell us the big news that she was pregnant. All her other friends were married and either pregnant or pointed in that direction, so she gave me a sheepish look when she made her announcement.

I think she even said something like, "Don't worry, Lisa; it will happen for you soon." I was nice about it, but I wish she'd known me well enough to realize that it really wasn't what I wanted. I think marriage and kids is one of those things that feels so natural to some people—like breathing or eating—that they can't imagine not needing it. They think you must be kidding yourself, or just pretending not to care.

It's not that I didn't want a relationship. I did want a steady partner—someone who cared for me, and whom I loved and respected in return. But the traditional way of having it wasn't anything that I dreamed about. I'd happily go along with my friends while they shopped for engagement rings. I remember I even called a friend one time when I spotted a ring in a window that I thought she'd like. But there was no vicarious thrill for me in doing that. It wasn't like I was taking notes for future me.

When my sister Andrea got married, and then my two close girlfriends from high school got married too, I was happy for them. I was also happy to buy a new dress, and to go to a big party with an open bar and fun music. But I definitely never thought, *When's my turn?* or *Now I need to find someone, too.* I never felt sad, or that I was missing out. Maybe I was permanently dissuaded from marriage by my parents' toxic union, but I think at a certain point you have to own your decisions. For whatever reason, I just didn't have the marriage chip.

Which isn't to say that I didn't sometimes feel like the rocky third wheel at weddings. It got kind of tiresome always being relegated to the "singles table"—you know, the one table where they stick everyone who isn't already married. The only thing that this motley crew had in common was that they weren't paired off. I always felt like I was on the wedding version of the Island of Misfit Toys. Initially I'd make conversation about how we all knew the bride or groom. Before long, I was drowning myself in champagne and pigs in a blanket. I was very good at playing the part of the happy wedding guest, but I felt like the extra in a movie. I put my hair up and wore a pretty outfit, but I was just window dressing, not really a part of the scene. It was a job. And at the end of the night I was happy to go home and take off my "Extra #1 Wedding Guest" outfit.

Over time, I found myself gravitating more toward my single friends. This was definitely the case once my friends started having babies. As much as I loved my friends with kids, and I loved their children, too, I just have to say this: children's birthday parties are not that much fun for single adults. There were only two elements of every child's birthday party that I liked and those were (1) pizza and (2) cake. But even the charms of melted cheese and frosted layers weren't enough of an incentive. I was grateful to my friends for wanting to include me, but I'd usually find that I was one of the only single people invited, and all the other adults were either married with kids already, married with a baby on the way, or married and thinking about getting pregnant—so they were perfectly happy to spend hours talking about all things baby- and child-related. Invariably, some mom who didn't know me would walk up and ask me if I knew the mother of the birthday boy from some mommy and me class, and I wanted to say that my whole life was a *me* class—forget the *mommy* part of it. "Me" was all I knew, and at that stage it was all I wanted to know.

So I avoided going to the children's birthday parties, which meant that I missed out on a lot of social occasions with my friends. Meanwhile, I know my married friends didn't invite me to all their adult gatherings—probably because they felt awkward about inviting one single girl to a dinner party full of couples. I get it now, but then I really didn't. Not having kids myself, I didn't understand why they couldn't talk about anything other than babies and babysitters and school. It seemed obsessive, like they'd lost themselves. I remember thinking, *What's going on here? How come I never see anyone?*

Just as I didn't always have as much sympathy for my friends as I might have, I did occasionally lose patience when people would ask me when I was going to settle down. It wasn't that I felt defensive, it was more that I wished they'd known me better and realized that I was doing really well already, and that I was on my way to my own version of happiness. I joke about my dating misadventures, but my work success gave me real joy, and I had wonderful friends, and I was already realizing a lot of the goals I had set for myself. How many other women in their twenties could say the same thing? So when I felt pestered by anyone, I just politely switched topics and said, "How about those Mets?"

Some people didn't get the hint and they'd keep pressing me. At a family gathering one time, an old friend of the family was eager to tell me all about her daughter, Marissa, and how happily married she was, and what a great provider her husband was, and how she was pregnant for the second time in two years, and how they'd just built a big, new house, and on and on. After all that, she looked at me insinuatingly and said, "So how about you, Lisa . . . anyone special?"

As proud of my work accomplishments as I was, it's still difficult to feel like people are judging you according to the rules of a game you're not even playing. It's hard to bite your tongue in those situations while trying to think of a polite way to say, "none of your business." But I realized that when certain women asked me about settling down, they were seeing me through their own dreams and choices. They shook their heads and felt sorry for me that I "still needed to work"—that is, that

I didn't have a man to take care of me. The irony of this was that a lot of the women I knew who'd relied on a man to take care of them found themselves disappointed in the long run. They might have picked a man that they thought could provide for them financially, but when things didn't work out, they felt abandoned. That wasn't what I wanted for myself. So I pledged early on that if I ended up finding Mr. Right, it wasn't going to be because of his money. Ambition was important to me, but as long as he could pay his own bills, the size of his bank account wasn't an issue. I may not have known exactly what I should be looking for in a man—at least not yet—but I knew that much.

This is my no-fail recipe. You can dump everything into a bowl at the same time if necessary (especially if you're headed out for a bootie call—no judgments here), and it will still come out delicious. Early on, I discovered the trick to these was to use store-bought cookie dough. Just add a warm coat over great lingerie and you can be on your way at a moment's notice.

Another great thing about this recipe is that the bars are best eaten frozen—they taste just like ice cream. So you can always keep a few stashed away for when the urge strikes.

HOW-TO-GET-A-MAN CHOCOLATE CHIP
CHEESECAKE SQUARES

1–2 rolls of store-bought
    chocolate chip cookie dough
    (see note)
2 8-ounce packages of cream
    cheese, at room temperature
1 cup sugar

2 eggs
1 teaspoon vanilla
8–10 ounces candy toppings
    (M&M's, toffee bits, chocolate
    chips, etc.), optional

Preheat oven to 350 degrees.

Line a 9 x 13–inch pan with parchment paper so that it overhangs
on the short ends of the pan—this way the bars will easily lift out
after baking.

Take slices of cookie dough (or crumble dough with hands) and
press together on the bottom of the pan to make one smooth
layer.

Mix cream cheese and sugar. Add eggs, then vanilla. Pour mixture
over the cookie crust and smooth with a spatula.

Top with any candy topping you like. *Note:* Alternatively, you
can use a second roll of cookie dough and place slices on top
of the cream cheese mixture to form another cookie layer. Don't
worry about neatness, the rounds will bake together here, and
looks aren't important in this recipe. You have other things on
your mind.

Bake for 30 to 35 minutes.

Let cool. Place in freezer until frozen, then remove from pan and
slice into 16 bars or 32 bite-sized squares.

CHAPTER 8

CEREAL MONOGAMY

I'd been happily freelancing for a while when I was offered a morning newsperson job at WNEW, the biggest rock station in New York City at the time. This was really the be-all and end-all of radio for me, and the station's DJs were like gods to me—that's how much I respected them.

I was teamed up with Richard Neer and Mark McEwen, two consummate radio professionals, and as always, it was like being thrown together on a blind date. *Okay, you total strangers go on and have fun—right now!* From the start, I adored Mark, and to this day he's someone I count on for support and honest feedback. Richard and I didn't get along quite so easily. He was one of those people who wanted to be the center of everything, the star of the show, and I was used to things being more collaborative. He had a very specific idea about how he wanted the show to be, and he wasn't going to have some relatively young woman come in and steal his thunder. He's not that much older than me, but somehow he seemed like he was from a different generation, and I got the feeling that he didn't much like having a woman on the air with him.

Mark, me, and Richard.

After a few years, WNEW decided to shake up their morning show and they broke up Richard and Mark and paired me with another experienced DJ, Dave Herman. He was pretty much cut from the same cloth as Richard. He'd already made a name for himself, and he clearly didn't get why he should have to share airtime with me.

This was one time in my life when my work situation correlated with my personal life—I was searching for the right mix, not always successfully, but I had faith that it was out there somewhere.

AFTER DAVID AND I broke up, I started getting a little more thoughtful about the kind of guys I was dating. I even started seeing some people who were genuine boyfriend material. I wasn't always ready to see them that way in the long term, but it was a step in the right direction for me.

My first semiserious boyfriend was intro-duced to me by my good friend Nadine. Michael was her husband's best friend, and he worked as an executive for a breakfast cereal company. I'd never had much luck with guys in ordinary nine-to-five jobs—I'd always found that kind of dull—but I decided to give him a try, and lo and behold, on our first date we clicked right away. Because he was an early riser too, he was completely fine with me needing to eat dinner at the same time as most eight-year-olds. In my experience, it was always the nice guys who were understanding and flex-ible with my hours. Unfortunately, I was rarely attracted to nice guys.

Michael was good-looking and kind, but he didn't excite me. This definitely wasn't any failing on his part—my issues were the problem, not Michael. The hottest sex we ever had was when we stayed overnight at his mother's house one weekend. We were supposed to stay in separate bedrooms, but he snuck me into his childhood room like we were a couple of teenagers. We had sex in his narrow wood-framed single bed and I remember the headboard actually heated up—not because our sex was so steamy, but because the kitchen stove was on the other side of the wall.

Michael was a lovely guy and we had fun together, but I felt like something was missing. To me, he lacked the spark of the unknown that I found so magnetic in other men. Of course, what I mistook for predictable other women might have seen as reliable. I think I actually saw decency and niceness as weakness. Based on what I knew, men weren't supposed to be sensitive and caring, and I didn't know how to react when they were. With men I was like a cat chasing down a mouse—I lost interest when my prey stopped fighting back.

Michael's social life revolved around a close circle of friends, and he worked really hard to maintain those friendships. His idea of a fun Saturday night was to have a small cocktail party for his circle, or to all meet at a restaurant. Now I realize I was scared to slow down and live in the moment, but back then I just felt bored and confined by the routine of his life. He'd want to make plans with me several days in advance so that he could coordinate everyone's schedules (the way adults do), but I still wanted to be a fly-by-the-seat-of-my-pants kid. I didn't want to plan a day in advance, much less a week.

My relationship with Michael was probably the healthiest I'd ever had, but it wasn't destined to last, and I couldn't give him what he needed or deserved—I was way too selfish at that point in my life. I wish there had been a guidebook I could have followed to tell me how to be a good girlfriend. You can't buy the simplest electronic device without getting a ten-page instruction manual, but no one ever gives you a manual before your first date with a new guy. Maybe certain things should have been obvious to me—maybe I shouldn't have needed to be told how to meet someone else halfway and to compromise, but it was all or nothing with me. Either I was hurling myself headfirst into a bad relationship, or I was keeping my heart under lock and key in a good relationship.

Michael once asked me to participate in a charity walkathon for a childhood disease that ran in his family, and I actually said no. I told him that I was a radio personality and I should have been hosting the walk, not walking in it. Of course he was upset, and he didn't try to conceal it, which surprised me—I never showed my own feelings so I didn't know what to do with a man who showed his. I was actually angry that he'd tried to make me feel bad about it, as if I were the one in the wrong. It was only later that I'd realize that he was asking me to be a supportive girlfriend and not a successful radio personality. At the time I wouldn't even acknowledge his feelings, and in fact I found his emotions kind of inexplicable. I'd never been with a man who was so up-front with what he was thinking and feeling.

In trying to bolster my own self-esteem, I had way over-course-corrected. I thought I was too big and important for Michael's rinky-dink walk-athon, and in the process I'd gone from being a self-perceived zero to being a fathead. But either way, my warped sense of myself all came from the same place—insecurity. I needed outside reassurance of my value, and it would take me a few years longer to get my head right.

My next victim was Jeffrey, a truly lovely man. We even met cute, at least from the perspective of a Jewish mother. I've always said that I didn't grow up with life lessons instilled in me—I couldn't spout off a single little gem of wisdom that was passed down to me at a young age. But the one bit of relationship advice I remembered one of my uncles offering me was to try flirting on the steps outside a synagogue. So I did.

I wasn't exactly devout, so it must have been a high holy day that brought me to my mother's Long Island synagogue—I think it was Yom Kippur. I batted my eyes at Jeffrey while we were both weak from hunger, and he took my number. He was a surgery resident at a hospital in Philadelphia, and even I, Miss Nontraditional, had to laugh at my luck in meeting a nice Jewish doctor at temple.

I thought he was smart and delightful. He made me laugh. He had a great smile, light eyes, and blond hair. As a resident, he kept his own crazy hours, so he was completely understanding about mine. In short, he checked off just about every item on my list of the perfect man. Except for one thing: there was no drama. He didn't leave me hanging, he didn't make me feel on edge, and he made it clear that he was looking for a long-term relationship. I didn't know what to do with that kind of clarity. But I also didn't want to break up with him, because I really cared about the guy.

I remember visiting him at work in Philadelphia and seeing him in action. I was so proud of him. It was the first time in my life that I felt that I could really love someone. I was deeply struck by what a wonderful human being he was.

That might have been our happy ending—or promising beginning—but, instead, that feeling of opening myself up to him utterly terrified me.

I stayed with him that night in his tiny resident's apartment. It was like being back in college in my eight-foot-by-eight-foot cell again. We tried to have sex in the shower, but we couldn't stand in there together and also move. We nearly broke the door. It should have been romantic—those could have been our salad days that we looked back on and told our grandchildren about when we were old and gray. But I didn't look at life that way—I didn't want to wait for my reward. I wanted to skip the work stage of things, wave a magic wand, and magically be where I wanted to be. I knew I had to work at my career, but somehow I got it in my head that I shouldn't have to work on a relationship. Spending the night in his little apartment should have been a bonding experience, but instead it felt like a letdown, like I didn't belong there.

I remember a friend of mine telling me what a great guy Jeffrey was for me, and how she thought he was really the one. But I couldn't see it at that point in my life. So when Jeffrey finished his residency and was offered a hospital job a few hours outside of New York City, I backed away and decided that we had to break up. I told him that our relationship couldn't last. I had to be in New York City to do my job, and long-distance relationships never work in the long term. . . . Excuses, excuses, each one lamer than the next. But I think Jeffrey knew the truth, that I was actually ambivalent about him. And for someone who was so sure of what he wanted, that was the kiss of death.

After we broke up, I had second thoughts, but at that point it was too late. He didn't want to have anything to do with me, and I couldn't blame him. Later I'd find out that he married a girl who was ready in all the ways I wasn't, and who knew exactly what she wanted—she wanted a husband and a provider, and she wanted to be a wife. I genuinely wished them both the best, and I tried not to regret the choice I'd made.

AFTER JEFFREY, I CONTINUED the serial monogamy phase of my dating life. I dated some good guys, some crazy guys, and some guys who seemed good and turned out to be crazy.

I tried some younger guys who were still figuring things out, like Brad, whom I met at my gym. He was very sweet and extremely good-looking, but he had no idea what he was doing in his life. Meanwhile, what he lacked in ambition he made up for in muscles. The first time he took off his shirt, the sight of his six-pack actually intimidated me, and in a weird way, it was a turnoff. Call me insecure, but I like to feel like I have a better body than my boyfriend. When we had sex, I was worried he'd spot some cellulite that I didn't know about. And when he asked me if I wanted to go to the gym with him, I wasn't sure if it was because he wanted to spend time with me, or because he was giving me a hint that I needed some exercise.

Then there was Foster, who got one question wrong on his SATs but was completely emotionally stunted. He was like Rain Man—his brain worked like a computer, but he didn't realize that it was considered rude to eat with both hands at the dinner table. He worked in finance and was incredibly bright and I admired his mind, but when he started drawing investment diagrams on the back of a paper napkin at a cocktail party, my eyes crossed. Not to mention, I couldn't take him out to restaurants.

While things with Jeffrey didn't end well, I had to admit that there was something to be said for dating a nice Jewish boy, so for a while there I did the whole Jewish dating circuit, going to all the singles events. I met Spencer at a Sabbath dinner, and we dated a few times, but he was so boring, so mind-numbingly stupid that even though he was a perfectly nice guy I would have sooner gone steady with Ted Bundy. I walked out of Spencer's apartment after our third date, and when he said, "I'd like to see you again," I actually burst into tears. It wasn't because I was sad, but because I realized it would be cruel to tell him that he was too dumb to date. I remember I felt so bad about the whole thing that I made him cookies.

I even dated an Orthodox guy at one point. He was very handsome and came from a huge family of ten kids. I stayed over at his place a few times, and unlike some men who told you they had an early meeting as a way of shoving you out the door, each time he was in a rush to go to early services. He kept strictly kosher, and when I added that fact to the number of babies his mother had brought into the world, I thought to myself, *Who am I kidding?* I eat spareribs on the Sabbath. I never met a lobster I wouldn't consume with relish. In his eyes, I wasn't even a Jew. He probably thought of me as his shiksa girlfriend.

If I had to come up with my funniest dating story, I guess it would be a tie between (1) the blind date who took a Quaalude before dinner and actually nodded off in his spaghetti (I kid you not: facedown in his plate of pasta) and (2) the man my sister fixed me up with who turned out to be an ex-con. Actually, I think number two wins by at least a nose. Just try keeping a straight face while your date tells you about his criminal drug record. It's not easy. I realized at that point that there was a limit to the drama that even I was looking for in a relationship. No fingernail files baked into layer cakes for me. I had to draw the line somewhere.

This cookie recipe has a lot of versatility, and what you add to it can really depend on who you're making the cookies for. If you feel like you're going bananas because your guy won't commit, by all means add Banana Nut Crunch. If your boyfriend is a real jackass, then Apple Jacks would be perfect, and maybe you should eat them yourself—he doesn't deserve cookies. If you want to drop a big hint and tell your guy that you're ready to go all the way, mix in some Lucky Charms. You get the drift.

FRUITY PEBBLES COOKIES

½ cup (1 stick) unsalted butter, at
  room temperature
½ cup packed light brown sugar
¼ cup sugar
¾ teaspoon vanilla extract
1 egg
1 cup all-purpose flour

½ teaspoon baking soda
2 cups Fruity Pebbles cereal,
  divided

2 large parchment-lined cookie
  sheets

Preheat oven to 375 degrees.

Cream butter and sugars. Add vanilla. Add egg and blend well.

In a small bowl, stir together flour and baking soda, then mix into the wet ingredients. Now add one cup of the cereal and mix lightly, just until distributed.

Using a small ice cream scoop, scoop out dough onto prepared cookie sheets, about 2 inches apart. Now take your remaining cup of cereal, and place a small pinch of it on the top of each cookie, lightly pressing down until just slightly flattened.

Bake 10 to 12 minutes, until just slightly golden at the edges.

Let cookies cool on rack.

Makes 30 small cookies.

CHAPTER 9

LOVE AT FIRST SIGHT

Some women cry over men. Some cry over the bathroom scale or the dressing-room mirror. Some can work up tears over television commercials. I tend to keep my emotions to myself—maybe to a fault—but I will cry over a broken heart. The time I cried the most wasn't over some guy, though. It was over a job—a dream job. A job I loved more than I'd loved any man up to that point.

When I joined Hot 97, it was the dance-music sister station to Kiss FM. I was hired to be the newsperson for the morning show, and I was excited about it. This was when I officially changed my on-air name to Lisa G. I'd never really loved my full name—I didn't think it sounded great on radio and people always struggled to spell it. I wanted something fresh and easy to remember . . . and I've been Lisa G. ever since.

Unfortunately, very soon after I started, the program director made it clear to me that he hadn't hired me for my personality. He told me I was "just a newsperson." Meaning, he wanted me to write my news reports, read them on-air, and not expect to banter with the hosts the way I'd always done. Luckily, that situation didn't last. A new program director came on board and he had the brilliant idea to bring in Doctor Dré and Ed Lover, former cohosts of MTV's *Yo! MTV Raps*. Around this time, hip-hop was just beginning to become more mainstream, and despite the fact that an enormous number of New Yorkers listened to hip-hop, it was still considered a fringey, outsider kind of music to a lot of the traditional media. So the fact that Hot 97, a major market radio station, was going to devote its morning drive-time radio show to hip-hop music was a really big deal.

Dré and Ed were already celebrities and tremendously knowledgeable about the music, but they'd never hosted a major market morning radio show before. So the program director wanted me to show them the ropes. Suddenly, my chains were off—I was back in local radio again, and they wanted my personality to come out. I felt liberated. There was no set of rules for us to follow because no one had ever really done this kind of morning radio before. So we just kind of made it up as we went along, and we decided to sound just as new and different as we actually were—because why have a hip-hop show if we were going to do everything the same as all the other stations?

My coworkers now make fun of me when I tell them stories about my days at Hot 97. They just don't

ED LOVER   DOCTOR DRE   LISA G   **HOT97**™

believe me when I tell them how huge we were. But if you weren't in the city then, or you weren't listening to hip-hop radio, you cannot know what a phenomenon that show became. One afternoon at the height of our success, I was walking out of Macy's after doing a little shopping, and a mob of teenage girls saw me from down the block. They ran toward me while screaming their heads off, totally surrounded me, then begged me for my autograph. It was the closest I'll ever come to knowing how Paul McCartney felt in 1964. The only difference was that our audience was black and Latino kids from Harlem, Brooklyn, and the Bronx.

At that point, music radio was still very much stuck in the old ways of doing things. In contrast, we were reaching out to the black and Latino youth of New York City in a way that no other station really did. We were a station that reflected the demographics of the city, playing the music that the city actually listened to in the clubs and in their cars. Back before you could listen to the radio on the Internet, people would actually tape-record our show and send it to their friends around the country. And entertainers and politicians who wanted to reach that untapped audience wanted to be on our show because they knew the power we had. In one two-hour window we could have on a rap artist, a movie star, Johnnie Cochran, and Jesse Jackson.

The combination of me, Ed, and Dré could so easily have failed. We could have not gotten along, we could have had zero chemistry. I could have tried too hard to sound like I was a homegirl, and they could have rolled their eyes at me and not taken me seriously. Instead, it was love at first sight and we all had a blast. It was the most fun I'd had on the radio since I started my career. Ed and Dré took to me right away, because I didn't pretend to know as much about the music as they did, and I made it so obvious that I was ready to learn. They knew that I wasn't trying to be anything other than who I was, a Jewish girl born and raised in Long Island.

I think that's a big part of why we worked so well together. Dré said to me recently that our differences made for great radio. He liked to joke that we were from opposite sides of the tracks, and he and Ed were always teasing me about the differences between white people and black people. He loved to say that white people were so crazy that when there was a hurricane at sea, we'd all run to the beach to look at it, and then get washed away by a wave. Meanwhile black people had the sense to run in the opposite direction.

I was just as willing as Ed and Dré were to talk about anything. When I got on the mike and freestyled with them or sang badly with one of our guests, it was hilarious. One time Ed said, "Who told Lisa she could sing if she just focused? The only way Lisa could sing is if she focused on another singer." I followed that put-down by trying to hit a high C on-air. It wasn't pretty, but it was definitely entertaining. Another time Ed said that guys were always asking him to set them up with me because I sounded so sexy, so he decided to try to auction me off on-air.

I'd bring in my dating stories, they'd bring in theirs, and they'd try to get me to tell them how good I was in bed. My boobs came up in one conversation and I told them that my cleavage had its own website. Dré said that the URL was www.wherearethey.com. So then we all said Dré's boobs were bigger than mine. It was back and forth like that all morning, every single day. We'd bust on each other and give advice like two black brothers and their Jewish little sister.

The whole atmosphere at the station was the perfect combination of close-knit family and creative excitement. I couldn't believe that I was working right across the hall from the fabulously smooth and soulful Isaac Hayes, who did the morning show for Kiss FM that aired opposite ours. He'd tell me fantastic music industry stories, and in return I'd steal his organic popcorn. This was back when it was really difficult to find and I'd grab any opportunity to snag some of his. He started calling me "the popcorn bandit," which makes me laugh to this day.

I REMEMBER THE HARDEST thing about morning radio, especially during my days at Hot 97, was just to try to make myself look presentable in the morning. The show aired from 6 A.M. to 10 A.M., so I had to be at the studio by 5:15. I'd power down some coffee and a bagel and then it was a marathon, no stopping. I had to wear glasses, because my eyes would be too puffy to get my contacts in, and I definitely wasn't camera ready. Meanwhile, we had a constant flow of celebrity guests.

Singing along with the guests became a running joke for me. My two favorites were Barry White and Tom Jones. There I was with two men known around the world for their deep, sexy, rich voices and I screeched along beside them to "Can't Get Enough of Your Love" and "What's New Pussycat?"

I did not sing along with Shaquille O'Neal when he came in, although come to think of it, that would have been pretty funny. In addition to being just as silly as you'd think, he was truly the tallest man I have ever seen in my life. I could have taken a picture of the two of us side by side—he's seven foot whatever and I'm five foot three. But that would be trite. So I took a picture of our feet instead.

I'd always loved the way radio stations felt like families, and I'd enjoyed joking around with the on-air staff at all my various jobs. But Dré and Ed took that to another level. Everyone who walked into that studio was treated like family, and they treated the fans the same way. I learned a lot from them about how to be more open-minded and to just enjoy people, even total strangers. We did a ton of promotional events after hours, and Ed and Dré loved the fans, loved talking to them, and they had no sense of entitlement. Unlike the kind of people that I grew up with in the wealthy Long Island suburbs, Ed and Dré didn't take their success for granted. They remembered where they came from. Some of their natural warmth and charm started to rub off on me, and I found myself opening up to fans more, and really stopping to listen and appreciate. I wasn't quite there with opening up to boyfriends yet, but in other ways, I was definitely becoming a better person.

While I'd always been pretty exclusively focused on getting ahead by working hard and keeping my eyes on the prize, I started to absorb the way a lot of Dré and Ed's popularity was sustained by friendship. They supported their friends no matter what, and their door was always open. I think that's why everyone loved them, including artists who'd already made it big and didn't really need Ed and Dré for a push. Will Smith, who had already made it big in *Independence Day,* would come by to promote a new movie, but instead of zipping in and out to do his interview like the typical celebrity would, he'd stick around just to hang with Ed and Dré. I look back on it now, and it's amazing to think of the people who would just stop by and ring the bell of the studio's private back door at six in the morning: Jamie Foxx before he was a big star. Tupac Shakur. Biggie Smalls. When Wu-Tang Clan came by, they'd bring their entire posse with them, and we'd end up with more than thirty people in the studio—it was like a packed train. Method Man drew a sketch for me that I ended up making into stationery.

Method Man's sketch.

Not all the artists who came by were easy. Mary J. Blige has come a long way since then, but when she first made it big and would come by the station for interviews, she was really difficult to draw out. She'd be all covered up in spandex and wearing sunglasses that she'd never take off. You couldn't see her eyes, so there was no way to read her mood during an interview, or to tell if she was even listening. Her handlers from the record company would stand around kind of looking at each other like, *Is it going to be a good day or a bad day?* When Ed asked Mary how the new album was going, the most we could get out of her was that it was "a lot of work." Period, that was it. Luckily Ed was a comedian, so he was good at filling dead air. And worst-case scenario, we could always go to a song.

In a million years I would never have predicted that just over a decade later Mary J. Blige would be breaking the all-time record for selling perfume on the Home Shopping Network. I find her story really inspiring. She proves that anyone can reinvent themselves and start over. I could also really relate to any of our guests who had substance abuse problems. My problem wasn't alcohol or drugs, it was emotional denial. But I was just as attached to my bad habits as any addict was. For years I was like the Hollywood sign—impressive from the front, but propped up and with nothing behind it. So I had a great deal of sympathy for anyone else who was trying hard to maintain a façade.

P. Diddy was another regular at the station, and he always came in with an entourage. His career was really taking off, and even at 7 A.M. he'd arrive looking like something out of a hip-hop *GQ* magazine spread. It seemed to me like there was a tornado of energy around Diddy, but it wasn't immediately clear whether it was good energy or bad energy. He would drop by out of the blue, but unlike some of the guys who'd come just to hang out, Diddy had an agenda—it was always, *play my music, play my music, play my artist, play my artist.* Push, push, push. He was a businessman at heart, and he never stopped working. The moral of that story is that you don't get as successful as P. Diddy by accident.

I was always really impressed by Queen Latifah as a person. She was breaking out of music and into TV and becoming a big celebrity, but she never lost her warm, local-girl quality. Whenever she'd come up to visit, she was a great interview, game for anything, friendly and professional. I had started doing some freelance work around that time and I reached out to her management to interview her for *Seventeen* magazine. There can be a lot of back and forth with management in those situations, and you end up wondering how difficult it could possibly be to get an artist to say yes or no. But with her management there was no drama or keeping me hanging, she said yes right away. When she did a special concert for Hot 97 at Webster Hall, I met her during a rehearsal break and she couldn't have been nicer. I always thought she had a fantastic singing voice, and I remember telling her that she should do an album of jazz standards. This was years before she did *Chicago*, so when she blew people's minds with her performance in that movie, I wasn't surprised at all.

LL Cool J was one of the guys who would just come by whenever he felt like it. He was a local boy from Queens and always so much fun on-air that it really felt like he was one of us. He agreed to let me interview him for a television show, and he could not have been more open and genuine. He even let us film him going back to his grandmother's house where his mother raised him. He showed us his room, which was a corner of the laundry room where they'd hung up sheets for walls. He pointed out his old electric drum pad where he made up his beats, and his bowling trophies and schoolbooks—everything was perfectly preserved and arranged, a little island of shelter frozen in a time capsule. It was incredibly sweet and touching, and I was also impressed by how much love and gratitude he had for his mother and grandmother. Like Ed and Dré, he was someone who never forgot where he came from and maintained a strong sense of who he was as a person.

I also loved Salt, Pepa, and their DJ Spinderella, who were our first guests when we started the show. They had a special relationship with our show after that, and they'd often fill in for Ed and Dré when they were traveling. Now it's commonplace for a celebrity to host an hour or sit in on a radio show, but in 1996 it was a very big deal. The energy of the show—which was normally filled with male humor—flipped when the four of us took over and all squeezed in behind the console. We'd call it ladies' day, and we talked about everything, including hair weaves and kids. In fact, once I was telling them how I thought they were superwomen, having these big careers and taking care of their kids, and then I had the bright idea to tell them that they should all bring in their kids the next morning.

All at once all three of them said, "Oh, no. It would be chaos."

Salt said, "Oh, Lisa, you don't want that."

Pepa said, "Lisa, you'd resign. All you'd hear on the radio is 'Tyran, no! Tyran, stop that!'" Then she told us all about how Tyran, her son who was probably about five or six at the time, had managed to make a $2,000 phone call to Japan from a limo one time. They teased me that only someone who didn't have little kids would think it was a good idea to bring them into a studio.

Their kids may have run them ragged at home, but you wouldn't have known it when they were in the studio. It amazed me how much energy they had in the morning, even if they'd been up late performing or promoting the night before. The running joke was that every five minutes or so Salt would say, "There's no place I'd rather be at 7 A.M. than on Hot 97!"

We had some great people in our studio, but of all the guys who came and hung out with us, the craziest and most lovable were Ol' Dirty Bastard and Flavor Flav. I became an adopted member of their wacky extended family—so much so that ODB and Flavor Flav would constantly call me in the middle of the night when they'd gotten themselves into some mess. I don't know if they thought I was their mother, their sister, their aunt, or some combination of all three.

At the time, I was dating a real straight-arrow guy named Jed. He was a totally nice guy, and definitely not used to the kind of insanity that I experienced at work on a daily basis. So when the phone rang in the wee hours and it was some rapper telling me he'd just been arrested, Jed was not amused.

The first time it happened, it was Flavor Flav, and the conversation went something like this:

Me: Hello?

FF: Hey, Lisa, it's me.

Me: What? Who?

FF: It's me. Flavor Flav.

Me: (looking at the clock) Flavor Flav? It's 2:30 in the morning!

FF: Yeah, well, you know, sorry about that.

Me: What's going on? Where are you?

FF: Rikers.

Me: Rikers?!

And so on . . .

It might seem crazy that Flavor Flav was calling me from Rikers, because after all, what was I supposed to do about it? But in a weird way, it was actually responsible of him. He was often our guest reader for the traffic report, so he was just giving me a friendly heads-up that he wouldn't be making it in for work the next day.

For some reason, it was always 2:30 in the morning when I got calls like this. Once it was ODB calling to tell me that he'd been arrested for stealing sneakers in Virginia. He was slurring, obviously still high, and insistent that he was innocent. He didn't need me to bail him out, he just wanted me to know, and he wanted me to tell Ed and Dré when I went to work the next morning. So when I got up for work two hours later, I propped my exhausted eyes open and passed on the news to Ed and Dré like I was a loyal sister protecting my naughty kid brother at the breakfast table.

With all these rappers coming by, some of them wasted, some of them not, it was my idea to have a "you know what I'm saying" bell. Every time one of the rap artists said, "you know what I'm saying," I'd ding a concierge bell. Depending on their level of sobriety, "you know what I'm saying" could easily be every other sentence and that bell would be clanging all morning like Notre Dame at midnight. But by far the most popular segment on our show was something we called "Roll Call." A listener would call in, we would freestyle a line, then the listener would fill in a line, and we'd go back and forth from there. People were obsessed with the Roll Call, and our phone lines would be all lit up like Christmas even before the show started. Even the celebrities were obsessed. Someone would come by to promote a new album and they couldn't wait to get on the mike to do the Roll Call. Celebrity encounters now are all so scripted. They do a satellite tour and get the same stupid questions over and over. But this was live, totally off the cuff and unpredictable, and they loved it.

One hip-hop star got just a little too comfortable with his surroundings. I didn't know Biggie

Smalls that well, and one day he was in the studio and he started rolling a joint during a commercial break. So I yelled at him like a horrified school-marm. "Biggie, you can't do that in here, we could lose our license!" Not to mention, it was 7 A.M. Biggie just kind of shrugged and smiled. "All right, Mom, no big deal."

I couldn't stay mad. Biggie was just being who he was, which was why he was so endearing to fans. I will never stop regretting that that was the last time I saw Biggie—I wish I could take back the scolding and that instead I had said something that better reflected how much I respected his work. It was a very short time later that I got a call from the station in the middle of the night. They needed me to come in and get on the air right away because Biggie had been murdered. The same thing had happened just a year before when Tupac was killed, and I couldn't believe that we'd lost another talented artist this way. Ed was out on the West Coast—not far from where Biggie was killed—so it was just me on the radio, and I opened up the phone lines so that heartbroken fans could call in. The outpouring of love was staggering.

ONE OF THE THINGS I most appreciated about working at Hot 97 was how racially diverse it was. The people working there—both on and off the air— really reflected the makeup of the city itself, and there were very few media outlets where you could look for that kind of accurate picture. Ed and Dré used to joke about the show *Friends* and wonder how a show like that, set in New York, could be so popular when none of them had black friends.

It is true that the rap and hip-hop world at the time was really heavily male dominated, and I was the only woman on-air at Hot 97 in the morning. But outside the studio, there were a number of African American women on staff with whom I became friends. Once the publicity department for the shoe company Lugz sent us a bunch of pairs of shoes. I must have said something about giving a pair to the guy I was seeing at the time, and one of my friends shook her head. "Oh, no. Never give a man shoes or he'll use them to walk out the door."

I said, "What are you talking about? I never heard that before."

All the women looked at one another, like *Doesn't this girl know anything?* The best advice my friend gave me, straight from her mother, was "Don't trip over dollars to get to nickels." Oh my God, how brilliant was that? And how true! How many times in my own life had I jumped across perfectly nice guys on my way to a bright, shiny jerk? Another saying I liked was, "Don't put your purse on the floor, because your money will walk away." I think that one works literally or figuratively. Either way, they're words to live by.

LIKE SO MANY PASSIONATE romances in my life, Hot 97 was destined to burn itself out. After five years, I thought we could have easily gone on for five more, but the powers that be had other ideas, and Ed, Dré, and I went our separate ways. I wasn't exaggerating at the start of this chapter—I cried real tears when this love affair ended. It was kismet, and I was so grateful every day I spent on that show. But better to have loved and lost, right? And now I knew what true romance really looked like.

I was constantly making cookies for the guys at Hot 97, so I had a hard time coming up with just one cookie that really reflected my time there. Then I realized something: to me, Hot 97 was the quintessential New York radio station—totally homegrown, fast paced, and spontaneous. And since black-and-white cookies are the quintessential New York cookie, it only made sense to include them here.

The typical New York black-and-white cookie, found in every self-respecting deli in the city, is easily 4 to 5 inches inches across. I like to make them smaller, and it doesn't make them any less delicious. If you want the classic supersized cookie, just add another 5 to 10 minutes of baking time.

BLACK-AND-WHITE COOKIES

For the cookies
1 cup sugar
½ cup (1 stick) unsalted butter, at
    room temperature
2 eggs

½ teaspoon vanilla
2½ cups flour
¾ teaspoons baking powder
½ cup milk

For the white icing
1½ cups confectioners' sugar
¼ teaspoon vanilla

⅜ cup milk

For the chocolate icing
1½ cups confectioners' sugar
¼ teaspoon vanilla
3 tablespoons unsweetened
    cocoa powder

⅜ cup milk

Offset spatula
Parchment-lined cookie sheets

Preheat oven to 375 degrees.

Mix sugar and butter until light and fluffy. Add eggs and vanilla. In
a separate bowl, mix together flour and baking powder. Add half
of the flour mixture to the butter and sugar mixture. Then add the
milk, and then the rest of the flour mixture. Mix until incorporated.

Using a small ice cream scoop, place heaping scoops of dough
onto the parchment-lined baking sheet, about 1 inch apart (space
them wider if you're making them larger).

Bake for about 10 minutes, until just starting to turn golden at the
edges.

Cool on wire racks.

Make the white icing first. Mix together the first two ingredients,
then slowly add the milk, using just enough to make the icing
easily spreadable. (If the icing gets too thin, you can add a bit
more sugar to thicken it again.)

Using the offset spatula, ice half of each cookie with the white icing. Allow to set for about 10 minutes.

Meanwhile, make the chocolate icing. Mix together the first three ingredients, then slowly add the milk as you did for the white icing. Now ice the other half of each cookie and allow to set before serving.

Makes approximately 48 small cookies.

CHAPTER 10

IF YOU BAKE IT, THEY WILL COME

My reputation now is that I'm little Miss Sugar Cookie who sits at home and knits and plays with my cat. One of the reasons I wanted to write this book is that whenever people assume those things about me I think to myself: *If they only knew.* For years and years, home was nothing special to me at all. The lease to my apartment had someone else's name on it. Even the furniture belonged to someone else. And when I wasn't working, I was out having fun. All I did in my apartment was sleep and have sex, so who cared what it looked like or how I felt about it?

Another reason not to get attached to home was that in radio I never felt like I could really plan ahead. People were fired and moved off to radio stations across the country all the time. It was like being in the military or working in professional sports—you never knew when you might be transferred or traded. I knew people who would check with their boss before they bought a house—they didn't want to sign on to a mortgage if their job was going to disappear in the next six months. To me, it seemed much safer to sublet an apartment than to make a commitment I might not be able to keep. I guess I had the same attitude toward real estate that I had toward men—I was always keeping my options open.

But just as I was starting to learn a little bit more about romantic commitment, I was beginning to see the appeal of having someplace that felt more like home. When I started at Hot 97, I was still living in my little studio alcove. But when things really started to take off, I felt like I could possibly do better for myself. So on a 100-degree day in the dead of a New York summer afternoon when every sane person was out of town, I went looking for apartments. I saw nondescript box after cookie-cutter box and nothing really moved me, until I walked into a one-bedroom apartment and I knew right away that it was the one for me. It had gorgeous prewar bones, wood floors, and it felt solid in a way that none of those other 1960s-era condos did. I took it on the spot. If only I could be so decisive with men, this would be a much shorter book.

I didn't exactly decorate my new apartment—I definitely wasn't thinking about color schemes or flipping through design magazines for inspiration. That was not my thing. But I took the major step (for me) of buying a few things from IKEA, and my mom gave me an old sofa and a coffee table. My desk was two filing cabinets with a board on top. I didn't paint or hang curtains or buy a bedspread. I just had your basic white vinyl blinds from Home Depot. My only investment was a new set of very basic baby-pink towels. And my one nod to decoration was a set of old Japanese prints that my grandmother had left me. I still love them to this day, but it's no coincidence that even when I had my own place I wasn't really asking myself what I wanted it to look like—I was letting circumstances decide for me.

You could definitely trace the way I came into my own through the furnishings in my apartment. It all started with hand-me-downs and cheap put-it-together-with-a-wrench stuff that wasn't designed to last. Then a really big step for me was to actually commission a furniture builder to make me an armoire for my clothes since I didn't have enough closet space. It was this huge gray thing made out of Formica, and in truth it was absolutely hideous, but it was indestructible and it was built exactly to my specifications. It was still solid and useful long after I'd realized it was ugly as sin. Finally, years later, I offered it to my building super, but it was so immense that he had to break it up with a crowbar to get it out of the apartment. We should all be so lucky as to invest our energy in something that serves us so well and never gives up.

It's also interesting to me that I had become the person who gives stuff to other people. First it was the armoire, and then it was a big leather sofa bed that had been my first major furniture investment, and which I gave to a coworker who was glad to have it. (He still jokes that he wishes he had a black light to shine on it and pick up the traces of all my sexcapades.) Is there anything more symbolic of growing up than getting rid of furniture that has run its course? Now I realized that I didn't have to settle for stuff that didn't suit me, any more than I had to settle for a man I didn't love. I didn't want to waste time, energy, or space on the wrong things—or people—anymore.

I KEPT UP MY baking for boyfriends, and now I was baking for everyone else, too. Baking became a way to relax and unwind after work, so I would bake even when I didn't have anyone specific in mind to bake for. I was always bringing in cookies for the guys at work, and if you ask any rapper who stopped into Hot 97 what they remembered most about me, at least one of the things would be my chocolate chip cheesecake brownies.

I truly loved to bake, which was really important for me, because ever since I'd given up my violin I had nothing to be passionate about other than work. Work was all-consuming, which was the way I wanted it. Slowly and surely, though, I was discovering that there was more to life than work, and that I was a person with more sides to me than the one that faced the microphone. It's funny, because around this time, a boyfriend asked me a question that left me momentarily speechless. On the radio, it was second nature to me to make a quick snarky reply no matter what question I was asked. It was a constant competition to see who could snap faster. But here I was, being asked a kind of serious question in my personal life, and I needed to think about it for a minute. It went against all my training to allow a few seconds of dead air. Finally my boyfriend saw that I was struggling for an answer and he said, "Do you need an on-air light?" That was amazing to me. Had I really become a person who was only "on" when I was on-air?

But back to baking. Even though I was still getting up before the roosters every morning (if there were roosters on the Upper East Side), I decided that I wanted to get better at pastry, and to really learn how the professionals did it. I guess I hadn't changed so completely from my workaholic ways, because I put my mind into baking the same way I did into my career—if I was going to do it, then I wanted to be really good at it.

Me and Bobby Flay.

I had become friendly with the chef Bobby Flay, whose Mesa Grill was one of the most highly regarded restaurants in Manhattan. I asked him if I could apprentice with his pastry chef, Alfred Stephens, on the weekends. Of course weekends were when I caught up on my sleep, so I was out of my mind to be doing this, but I jumped into it with both feet. And my God, I had obviously chosen to apprentice in one of the few jobs that was even more physically grueling than the one I already had. Added to the exhaustion of getting up early, as all pastry chefs do, was the sheer backbreaking labor of lifting huge bags of flour and massive trays out of hot ovens. It also seemed like everything in the kitchen was arranged for six-foot-tall men, so no matter what I needed, it was always about a foot over my head.

The original Kardashians.
Me, Bonnie, and Andrea.

Smiling and
on my own.
Something I'd get
used to.

Beginnings of a cat lady. My first cat, Taffy.

Me at age twelve with gazelle legs and rabbit teeth.

Lisa Glasberg - violin

Achievement	A	A
Effort	A	A
Attitude (remembering lessons, books and instrument)	A	A

Lisa does very, very well on the violin and is a pleasure to teach.

F. Schenkel

Parent's signature Mrs E. Glasberg

Look what the philharmonic missed out on.

**Newspaper
Indentification Card**

PRESS

LISA GLASBERG

Representing South Shore Record

THIS CARD FOR IDENTIFICATION ONLY

At age seventeen. While my friends were getting fake IDs, I got my first authentic press card.

High school
cheerleading
squad. Give me
a double D!

My first blog. Diary of a Mad
Insecure Cheerleader. Is it any
wonder I became a workaholic?

At five foot three, I was just
another peanut at Jimmy
Carter's inauguration.

Big eighties hair to match my big boobs.
© *by Marc Raboy*

Chicago radio. Hard to tell if I was hiding my dark
circles from an all-nighter or channeling Elton John.
© *by Paul Natkin/Photo Reserve, Inc.*

My freshman class photo from Hot 97. © *by Hot 97 FM, New York*

Universal Studios Florida with Flavor Flav. The biggest alarm clock that never worked.

Will Smith: the Fresh Prince of Bel-Air, with the Jewish Princess of Long Island.

Cher, post-*Moonstruck* and me, post–blonde dye job.

With Anthony Bourdain. You can never have too many chefs in the kitchen when you throw a cookie party.

P. Diddy, Pepa of Salt-N-Pepa, and DJ Jazzy Jew.

The Grammys. Winner of Best Reporter in High Winds and High Heels Atop a Mobile News Van.

Proud mom with her newborn.

Thanks to Paramount Pictures, the premiere for *Dinner for Schmucks* (here with star Zach Galifianakis) was the first red carpet where I didn't feel like one. © *by Michael Morales*

I never dreamed as a double-D-lister I'd get to interview an A-lister like Steve Carell. © *by Michael Morales*

At the *Sex and the City 2* movie premiere. Leaning on the barricade I would later jump over to interview Sarah Jessica Parker.

The other thing I did not love about my apprentice-ship was the quiet. When you think of kitchens and chefs, you picture everyone crowded in together and cursing like banshees. That, to me, is not so different from a radio station, so I would have been comfort-able in that environment. But pastry chefs usually work in silent, windowless basements, hours before any of the other cooks are even awake yet. By the time the rest of the staff is rolling in, the pastry chef is heading home.

I was critically exhausted while I was apprentic-ing and working full-time, and it was also winter, so I suspect I was a little light deprived, too. When I'd let myself take a nap in the afternoon, I'd wake up at 5 P.M. and it would already be dark outside. I'd jump three feet in the air thinking that I'd overslept my alarm clock. Heart pumping, it would take me a good few minutes to calm down and realize that it was evening and not dawn. Finally I realized that I had learned as much about pastry as I needed to, and I said my good-byes to that wonderful appren-ticeship. The physical torment aside, I learned a ton about technique and efficiency in the time I spent at Mesa Grill. And it's thanks to the confidence I gained that I launched my cookie parties.

The parties started out on a small scale, with just me and a few dozen of my closest friends. I made tons of desserts and served wine and champagne. It was cozy and celebratory, and I discovered that there was something really special about having people into my home and watching them gobble down goodies that I had made with my own two hands.

It did not take long, though, for cozy to turn into massive, and soon my cookie parties were huge bashes and I'd have a hundred or more people crammed into my one-bedroom apartment. That one hundred or so people would rotate over the course of the evening, so by the end of the night who knew how many hundreds of people had been there. I invited a core group of friends, and then they invited more, and then I invited near-total strangers, too. My friends always tease me that whenever I'm introduced to someone for the first time I say, "Hi. I'm Lisa. Wanna come to my cookie party?" I am constantly meeting people who tell me, "Oh, yeah, I went to one of your cookie parties," or "Oh, right, I ate brownies on your bed." Just recently I met someone who said, "You know, my dear friend James Gandolfini went to one of your cookie parties back when he was skinny and had hair." When I heard that, I can't tell you how fast I rushed back home to look through my pictures and hopefully find one of him leaning up against a door frame. No luck.

I had a winning formula for my cookie parties—great food, plentiful drink, and a nice mix of people. As the parties got bigger, so did my baking workload, until I was preparing for them weeks in advance. Every night in the days leading up to the party—after I'd already worked a full day at the station, mind you—I'd make desserts and freeze them in stacks. I always made at least two dozen of everything, from mini pecan pies to chocolate chip oatmeal cookies. By the end of the week my refrigerator looked like the makings of a diabetic coma. The night of the party, while I danced around my guests, I was also running a trail between fridge and serving tables, refilling and making sure everything stayed nice and chilled— because there's nothing worse than a soggy chocolate chip cheesecake square.

One year, I thought a good twist on the theme would be to celebrate chefs I had either come to know or knew about. A side benefit is that it would take some of the hard cookie labor off me. This was after I'd left Hot 97 and was working at WOR Radio. Cooking shows were really starting to boom, and WOR had a number of them, so it was a good tie-in to my work as well.

The first chef I asked was Alfred Stephens from Mesa Grill. I still remember his homemade Hostess cupcakes, and a banana cake layered with peanut butter buttercream and glazed with jelly. To die for. I also asked Erik Blauberg, the chef at the '21' Club (I nabbed him during an interview). He made opera espresso cakes and white chocolate mousse cups. I grabbed Jacques Torres when he was the pastry chef at Le Cirque. I was trailing him for an article I wrote for the *New York Post*, so of course I took advantage of the opportunity to have him throw his hat in the ring. He made a fig tart. Anthony Bourdain brought a layer cake. I had met him while I was eating at his restaurant Les Halles, and he was just starting to make a name for himself as a writer. I was thrilled when he came to the party, because I knew already that he was going to become famous. He had star power, it was obvious. Anyway, with all these chefs stopping by and bringing their amazing desserts, my little cookie parties were becoming like a mini Aspen food festival. I even convinced Veuve Clicquot to sponsor one of my parties, and this was long before anyone was doing that—definitely before every housewife, city or suburban, was lining up corporate sponsors for their Chihuahua's birthday party.

Speaking of housewives, as publicity for the parties started to grow, I got very good at picking out the people who were there just for the media exposure. One person whom I really considered a friend lost all sense of herself at one of my parties. That year, the party was being covered by the *New York Times*, and I noticed that she made sure she was in every photo op. If the cameraman's lens was pointing at the cheesecake bars . . . she'd be holding up a slice. If the camera was pointed at a cake, she'd make sure she was cutting into it. And when the reporter went around the room for quotes, of course she was front and center. She was not such a good friend after that.

An autumn cookie party.

By far the hardest thing about the cookie parties was how to avoid telling certain people that their pastry sucked. I appreciated the people who chipped in, but there were times when I'd get about ten different batches of brownies. For some reason, a lot of people think they can make the perfect brownie. In truth, it's probably one of the more difficult desserts to get right, because it's all about texture and timing. Some batches were burned and dried out; others were just ugly. I'd have stacks of these second-string sweets sitting in my kitchen, just waiting for their moment. I wouldn't put them out at first, but as I quickly learned, after a few stiff drinks a burned brownie can taste delicious. So I'd more than gladly take these misfits out of their tinfoil after a few hours and toss them on a serving plate front and center. Once the alcohol was flowing, my guests would eat anything. Melted cake, soggy pie, didn't matter. Which was good for me, because I never had leftovers.

Just recently I was looking at pictures from some of my first cookie parties and noticing the string of boyfriends that I had over those years. Some of them were more casual than others. There was the younger guy I met at the gym, a really cute personal trainer. Turns out he and I had grown up in the same neighborhood, and I teased him that as much of a musclehead as he was now, little old me had kicked sand in his face back then. Anyway, he was sexy and cute, and what a great body.

He was just the kind of guy that I would have thrown myself at just a few years before. I probably would have shown up at his door in nothing but a jog bra, holding a plate of chocolate chip cookies. Those days were finally over, though, and the cookie parties helped me realize that once and for all. Now I was baking for me, and as a way of showing my love, as opposed to trying to win someone else's. And that's a big difference.

In celebration of my big life in the Big Apple, I felt what better way to honor New York City than to create an apple pie cookie. I used to make mini apple pies for all my cookie parties, after noticing that no one wanted to slice a big piece of pie because it meant using utensils (and how can you hold a drink if you're standing and using a fork?). For this book I wanted the same delicious apple pie flavor

but in a cookie. I know Mayor Bloomberg wants everyone to cut down on snacks in his city, but I dare him to say no to these. If you want to get adventurous and further thumb your nose at calorie counts, place a scoop of vanilla ice cream between two cookies and then it's an apple pie cookie à la mode!

BIG APPLE (PIE) COOKIES

½ cup (1 stick) unsalted butter, at room temperature

½ cup white sugar, plus ½ teaspoon for dusting apples

½ cup packed light brown sugar

1 teaspoon vanilla

1½ cups all-purpose flour

1½ teaspoons cinnamon, plus ⅛ teaspoon for dusting apples

¾ teaspoon baking soda

¾ cup peeled, finely diced Granny Smith apples

½ cup chopped toffee

Parchment-lined cookie sheets

Preheat oven to 325 degrees.

Cream butter and ½ cup of white sugar until incorporated. Add brown sugar. Mix until fluffy. Scrape down sides of bowl. Add vanilla and mix again.

In a small bowl, stir together flour, 1½ teaspoons of cinnamon, and baking soda. Add to butter mixture and mix until dough looks like sand.

Sprinkle apple pieces with remaining ⅛ teaspoon of cinnamon and ½ teaspoon of sugar. Now fold apples and toffee pieces into dough.

With ⅜-ounce ice cream scoop, scoop out balls of dough. Space 2 inches apart on parchment-lined baking sheets. Press each cookie down slightly.

Bake for 18 to 20 minutes, until cookies appear firm and the surface starts to crack a little.

Makes 24 cookies.

CHAPTER 11

WHAT I LEARNED FROM TV

When I first started at Hot 97, the original program director had told me in no uncertain terms that I was "just the newsperson." I could have let that knock my ego flat, but instead I decided that I needed to make my own opportunities. If I didn't want to be "just the newsperson" on a radio station, maybe I needed a plan B—and C. People in media always have to have a backup plan, and I took the program director's lack of interest in me as a message not to put all my eggs in one basket. So that's when I decided to try my hand at television. I still loved radio, but I was looking for something extra to do in the afternoons for more exposure and income.

One of my freelancing jobs before Hot 97 had been in the news department at VH1. I was supposed to report and write for the on-air VJ, a woman who was really not the sharpest tack in the box. Pretty? Yes. Bright? Not so much. So here I was doing all this work to make her sound good (and smart) on TV, and I thought to myself: *I could do what she's doing.* I didn't kid myself that I was the greatest beauty in the world, but in comparison to her I realized that I had more to offer.

That experience gave me the confidence to make an audition tape. Then I called everyone I knew in media and told them what I wanted to do. Voilà, it worked. My first freelance job was for a show called *The Real Story* on CNBC, and it was a blast. It was a news story about the girls who danced in the background of rap videos, so not only did I interview the girls and go on location with the artists, but part of my story was to dance in the video rehearsal. It was so much fun, and exactly what I needed to feel like I wasn't "just a newsperson."

Very soon after that I was hired for a new local morning show called *Weekend Today in New York* on WNBC. The host was Bill Boggs, and I was brought in to be the entertainment reporter.

After years of working on the radio, I was used to having to beg artists for interviews. So the thing that struck me first about television was how incredibly easy it was to lure in celebrity guests. In comparison, getting celebrities on the radio was like pulling teeth. But *everyone* wanted to be on television—all you had to do was ask and you got them. On the one hand, this bizarre phenomenon made my TV job easier, but on the other I found it so frustrating. I was the same person whether I was on the radio or on TV, and tons of people listened to New York radio. Those stars should have been just as happy to be interviewed on Hot 97. But the visual of television was so magnetic to people, and I guess they felt that being seen *and* heard was much more worth their time than just being heard.

In any case, New York is such a big market that if celebrities were in town for a concert, or to promote their album, movie, or new television show, they came on *Weekend Today in New York*. I interviewed Jon Bon Jovi, Jewel, Cher, Diana Ross, RuPaul (I had to interview him while standing on a box because he was so tall), Dolly Parton (she and I were wearing the same shirt at the time, a jersey turtleneck with cutouts over the shoulders; it looked a little different on me), Michael Bolton, Barry Manilow, the Beach Boys. Let's just say that those were more familiar acts for the station to go after, as opposed to the hip-hop artists I interviewed on Hot 97. Of course, now any morning show would kill to have Jay-Z on, but back then hip-hop still seemed like a foreign language to them.

When I first started out on TV, I did all my hair and makeup myself, with no professional intervention. I had long hair, and I thought it was nice, but it really didn't have any style to it. Then I was offered a job as a correspondent for *The Gossip Show* on E! and I was told that perhaps I needed a little help in this area. The executive producer called me after one of my segments, and he said, "Lisa, we think you're terrific, but what's with your hair?"

I really wanted to succeed in television and I naively decided that if this guy worked with celebrities, then he must know what he was talking about. So I got my hair cut up to my chin. This was when bobs were really big, so I figured that's what I should get. Later, one of my friends said, "Lisa, why'd you go so extreme? He told you to get a style, not to cut it all off." But there was no halfway with me, and if he didn't like my hair, then I got rid of it. It's a good thing he didn't ask me to sleep with him.

After that not-so-great experience, I decided to get some truly professional help in the form of a stylist. This was a revelation. I learned so many things from him and my producer that had never occurred to me before:

1. **I have a freakishly large head.** But wait, you don't have to feel sorry for me, because apparently having a really big head is a good thing on TV. It fills the screen. And if you put really big shoulder pads in all your tops, it helps to minimize the enormity of your skull.

2. **My eyes are lopsided.** Do not go on television if you have any tendencies toward body issues (that was a joke— who doesn't have a tendency toward body issues?). The camera causes you to dissect your own face to a degree that is insanity inducing. This must be the cause of all the plastic

surgery in Hollywood. In my case, after staring at myself in the mirror for hours, I discovered that my eyes are crooked.

3. **My lips are also kind of wonky.** See above. But here's a neat trick a makeup artist taught me: you can correct this imbalance with lip liner. Just be careful you don't start looking like an old-timey movie actress. The producers don't like that, and it scares the kids watching at home.

4. **Don't wear prints.** They're hypnotizing, and not in a good way.

5. **Don't wear anything with too much stretch.** It shows bulges.

6. **Fake eyelashes are a godsend.** When I tried these the first time, suddenly my eyes looked huge! They still looked lopsided, unfortunately, but you can't have everything.

7. **Soft lighting is your friend.** And so are the guys who adjust your lighting for you. Some days when I was feeling less than fresh, the lighting guys were the only thing keeping me from looking like an extra on *The Walking Dead*. Thank you, lighting guys, I will love you forever.

8. **The right bra makes all the difference.** So does double-sided tape.

9. **Bright colors pop on camera.** They make you look awake! However . . .

10. **Be careful with lipstick.** Pink is not my color; neither is coral. But MAC Viva Glam lipstick—the first one—is awesome.

Finally, there's one more thing I learned from television that my stylist didn't teach me but that I picked up everywhere I went: you're never young enough. No matter how young you are, or think you are, or how young you feel, someone else is always going to be younger.

Blond as can be.

TELEVISION IS FUN AND chaotic, and if I thought it was stressful to have to fill airtime on the radio, I did not know stress until I added on the whole visual component of TV. I remember I did some freelance work for ESPN2, covering the New York City Marathon. When you're on-air, you have these little tiny earbuds so you can get instructions from the producers. I was used to that, fine. But what I wasn't used to was having the producers literally *screaming* into my ears for the entire time I was on-air. They were cursing and carrying on like the *Hindenburg* disaster was unfolding over our heads. Afterward, one of the screaming producers told me what a great job I'd done, and I thought to myself, *This is bananas.* Fabulous, absolutely. But bananas, definitely.

And that's why I love TV. Because if you're a girl who thrives on a challenge, excels under pressure, and likes to have someone else do her hair and makeup . . . there's really nothing like it.

I had to pick blondies for this chapter—the thematic linkage is just too perfect. When I first started working on TV, something very important about me changed: my hair color. I became blonder and blonder. But there was a method to this madness. I realized very quickly that my naturally dirty-blond hair didn't read well on TV. It looked brown or reddish brown, and not in a good way—this was in more of a dull-as-dishwater way. So I looked around and noticed that a lot of the women around me were very, very blond. So I took a cue from them, and the lighter I went with my hair color, the better I looked on TV, too. Unfortunately, after a few years of this, my hair was a fried mess, and I eventually found a wonderful hairdresser who got my hair back to its natural shade. Hopefully all those years of peroxide didn't kill too many of my brain cells. It's a good thing this recipe is so easy.

BLONDIES

¾ cup (1½ sticks) unsalted butter,
  at room temperature
1 cup light brown sugar
½ cup sugar
2 eggs
2 teaspoons vanilla
1½ cups all-purpose flour

1 teaspoon baking powder
¾ cup butterscotch chips
½ cup semisweet chocolate chips

9 x 13–inch pan lined with
  parchment paper, overhanging
  on the short ends

Preheat oven to 350 degrees.

Cream butter and sugars until fluffy. Add eggs and vanilla and beat thoroughly.

In a small bowl, mix together flour and baking powder, then add to the butter mixture until there are no white streaks. Now mix in all the chips. Spread evenly in the prepared pan.

Bake 25 to 30 minutes, until edges turn a little golden brown.

Makes 32 one-and-a-half-inch squares.

CHAPTER 12

BAKER'S RACK

You can tell yourself that your brain is the most important thing about you—or your soul, if you're spiritual. But realistically, it's our bodies that we carry around the world with us for all to see. It's our bodies that everyone judges on first meeting (whether they think they're the judgmental type or not). And for most women, it's how that body of ours looks in the morning that tells us whether it's going to be a good day or not.

If you ask everyone you know to tell you one physical characteristic that has defined them, you're going to hear a bunch of different answers. Height, weight, the size of their noses, whatever. And for a lot of people, that characteristic was something that emerged suddenly, crazily, even aggressively, in adolescence (gazelle one year, giraffe the next; Taylor Swift one year, Barbra Streisand the next). For women across the board though, I would argue that nothing affects our physical self-image more than the size of our boobs.

Guys may worry about how they measure up, too, but unless the man in question is Michael Fassbender, that information is rarely made public. I'm sure there's some comparison shopping done at urinals, despite the fact that men insist that they don't look. (Do you believe them? I don't.) And we all know that guys love to brag about the size of their packages. But that's not the same thing as entering a room, fully clothed, and having everyone be able to make an approximate guess as to what bra size you wear and whether they're real or not.

Speaking of real versus augmented, I've often noticed that the women who come into their boobs early on tend to spend a lot of years hiding them. Maybe later on they learn to flaunt what they've got, but if you were the only girl in your sixth-grade class wearing a support brassiere, you were probably also wearing a lot of turtlenecks and hunching your shoulders. The girls who spent some portion of their lives flat chested and who sprouted later—either for free or bought and paid for—tend to be prouder about showing off their cleavage.

I definitely fell into the former category. My mom was slender and willowy, and my sisters were the same. But somehow I ended up inheriting my grandmother's eastern European zaftig gene. I swear I saw one of my grandmothers pull a full-sized change purse out of her brassiere. She kept everything in there—spare tissues, you name it. She would have slaughtered the competition on *Let's Make a Deal*. There's not a thing Monty Hall could ask for that she couldn't have pulled out of her bra. Both my grandmothers wore bras with complex engineering to rival the George Washington Bridge. So there I was with a small build like my mother, but these boobs like my grandmothers', and I had no idea what to do with them. My mother didn't know what to do with them either. She actually gave me my older sister's hand-me-down training bra. Besides the fact that my sister and I were built completely differently, I would argue that your first bra is something that you want to be able to cut the tags off of yourself. Hand-me-down coats I understand, but a hand-me-down bra? Not so special.

Me and Andrea with my grandmother Fanny.

Me with my grandmother Muzzy.

I swear my boobs sprouted overnight, like some-one gave me a pill and, boom, there they were. I was like those boys who start high school at four feet tall and when they graduate they're six foot three. In high school I'd hide my boobs behind my books. By the time I got to college I was a 32C, and my tactic changed. At my work-study job in the office of the communications department, I'd make sure I posi-tioned myself so that the typewriter was in front of me. That way I figured I wouldn't look like a head attached to two boobs, which is how I felt.

The boobs-with-a-head look was a-okay with the guys I dated, but the practical problem was that I couldn't find 32C bras in those days. Bras were either big and wide all around, or dainty and lacy and non-supportive. There was nothing in between, at least not in the stores where I shopped. Maybe if I went to some high-end boutique on Madison Avenue I would have found something, but that wasn't my speed in those days. So either I didn't wear a bra at all, which was really uncomfortable, or I had to try to custom-ize the wrong-sized bras I had.

This was when I turned into an amateur seam-stress. Very amateur. I'd buy 34B bras, and I'd perform major surgery on them, all by hand. I'd cut and resew the strap so it fit me better around the rib cage, but then there would be buckles and bulges everywhere else. Not pretty. Trying to find clothes that fit was also a trial. Everything was small on the top or too big on the bottom. Forget trying to find a dress. I had to buy two-piece everything so that I could get the tops in a larger size than the bottoms. I think that's one of the reasons I was so excited when I found my magic purple jump-suit—a one-piece article of clothing that fit me was the fashion equivalent of Ahab's white whale.

It wasn't until years later when I went to Paris for the first time that I realized I had discovered bra nirvana. There were 32C bras everywhere—hanging in the grocery store right next to the toothpaste. I couldn't believe it. The laciest, most beautiful bras were lined up at checkout, and Frenchwomen could buy them in the same place they got their milk and laundry detergent. This, to me, is why Frenchwomen are different. It's not the red wine and cheese diet. It's that they never have to cut up and resew their bras. No wonder they're so disgustingly confident.

I'm not complaining about having big boobs. I loved that guys were excited by my surprise reveal when I took my clothes off. I remember when one boyfriend saw me naked the first time, he looked at my boobs and said, "Holy shit, Lisa, where have you been hiding those?" I had to laugh, because it's true that I spent most of the time keeping my boobs under wraps. I felt like *Wizard of Oz*–era Judy Garland, when the studio chiefs insisted she bind her breasts with tape so she'd look younger and more innocent. I did my own version of breast-taping (unfortunately, none of my old outfits will be sold for hundreds of thousands of dollars the way Dorothy's dress was). Radio was a really male-dominated field, and I wanted to be taken seriously. I didn't want the lecherous old station manager leering at me or staring down my shirt. And I definitely didn't want people in the business to think that my looks were more important than what came out of my mouth. In general, I felt like I had an uphill battle in trying to be taken seriously, and my boobs were just one factor. Men of a certain generation did the hiring, and they tended to favor other men, and they figured that a nice, pretty, Jewish girl like me from the suburbs of Long Island wasn't exactly a force to be reckoned with. So I wore a lot of turtlenecks.

PHOTO BY HOWARD STERN.

Flash forward a few years, and I went for a bra fitting at one of those fancy lingerie boutiques that I didn't even know existed when I was back in college. The salesperson was a full-figured middle-aged woman with sure hands and a tape measure, and she told me with definitive authority that I'm not a 32C at all. I'm a 30D. Put this in the category of: learn something new every day.

Now I don't hide my boobs as much as I did back in the day, but I'm still not one to advertise them. When my bra size comes up in conversation (and I have to tell you, it's surprising how often this happens), people have a hard time believing that I'm a 30D. They think that with those measurements I should look like a porn star. So this picture is my little gift to all the naysayers. Or just call it an "I told you so."

This is the type of recipe you can pass on to your girlfriends. Unlike a training bra, this cookie is definitely one size fits all. I've never met anyone who didn't love it. It just busts out with flavor (get it?). And it's endlessly customizable, so feel free to substitute dried cherries, raisins, and flavored chips for the last two ingredients.

DOUBLE D-LICIOUS OATMEAL COOKIES

1 cup (2 sticks) unsalted butter, at
   room temperature
¾ cup granulated sugar
¾ cup light brown sugar
1 egg
1 teaspoon vanilla extract
1½ cups all-purpose flour

1 teaspoon baking soda
1½ cups oatmeal (not instant)
¾ cup dried cranberries (I use
   Craisins)
1 cup white chocolate chips

Parchment-lined cookie sheets

Preheat oven to 350 degrees.

Cream butter and sugars until fluffy. Add egg and vanilla until
incorporated. In a small bowl, mix together flour and baking soda,
then combine with butter mixture.

Fold in oatmeal until fully incorporated, then dried fruit and chips.

Using a ⅜-ounce ice cream scoop, scoop out balls of dough onto
parchment-lined cookie sheets, spacing 2 inches apart. Push
down on cookies slightly.

Bake 10 to 12 minutes, or until cookies start to turn a pale golden
brown at the edges. Do not overcook! Cool on a rack.

Makes approximately 43 cookies.

CHAPTER 13

WHY CAN'T YOU GET A JOB LIKE EVERYONE ELSE?

I met Andrew at the gym. I'd first noticed him on Fire Island on summer weekends, so when I ran into him at the Vertical Club, he looked familiar to me already. Meanwhile, I want you to know that we were definitely not the only ones looking for love among the fitness machines. That gym was like a nightclub with marginally more Lycra.

A friend introduced us in the lobby, and we hit it off right away. It helped that I thought Andrew was adorable. He had a tennis racket under his arm at the time, and he was built like a tennis player, which I loved. I'd had romantic notions about tennis players ever since summer camp. He had a great smile, and he showed it a lot because we spent a good portion of that first conversation laughing. I couldn't remember the last time I'd clicked with someone like that—it was chemical, definitely, but it was more than that. He seemed like the kind of guy who wouldn't be a lot of work and drama. He seemed easy—in a good way.

We became serious pretty quickly, and I remember that he introduced me to his family really fast. He worked in their very successful real estate business, and we spent a lot of time at their beautiful house in New Jersey. I loved the house and I was impressed by how close-knit his family was, but at the same time I couldn't imagine my family being so tied up with my work life. It seemed . . . suffocating.

They all ate, drank, and slept the family business, and they went to the country club together, and they were always networking with other wealthy, high-powered people. They were all blond, too, which was kind of amazing. They were like the poster family for Ralph Lauren, which is perfect because they were Jews trying to look like WASPs, and they associated with other similarly attractive family dynasties. They really didn't stray far from their comfort zone, and to his family—especially his mother—I was a *big* step outside.

We had a lovely time together—for a while—but after a certain point, our different outlooks started to cause friction. I considered myself self-made at work, so I don't think I was as supportive of Andrew's work as I could have been. Being in a family business has its own special set of daily stresses, but I had a hard time sympathizing. It seemed to me like he had it pretty easy, and I suspect I didn't hide that too well. Meanwhile, his family couldn't understand my career and my unusual hours. To Andrew's mother I probably seemed one cut above an exotic dancer. During a family dinner, she turned to me and said, "Why can't you get a job like everyone else?"

I was so hurt. I'd worked so hard to get where I was. She seemed to think that just because my hours were strange and my job was to sound happy and entertaining, I wasn't actually working. What was really underlying her question, though, was a judgment about how important my career was to me. That's not what she wanted for her son. She wanted him to have a wife who would always put him first. I couldn't really blame her, but that wasn't me. What upset me more than Andrew's mother's comment was the fact that Andrew hadn't stuck up for me.

Our relationship was already unraveling when Andrew and I decided to go to Hawaii. There's nothing like a romantic vacation to either cement or destroy a relationship. For us, it was definitely the nail in the coffin. We were in this beautiful place, and it only served to shed harsh light on how unhappy our relationship was. We looked around us at other well-matched couples enjoying the sand and pristine water, and it was so obvious that we weren't like them. The whole time we were there I was miserable, and I'm sure he was, too. Even when we had sex, it was unsatisfying. It was breakup sex without the sexy part. I just wanted to leave paradise, get on a plane, and go home. When we got back to town, we broke up. He said that I wasn't "the one." I couldn't disagree with him.

Unhappy in Hawaii.

And I guess I wasn't surprised when I found out that six months later he met the woman he'd marry. She looked kind of similar to me, which somehow made it harder, and she quit her job soon after the wedding. Career wasn't even in the running for the most important thing in her life.

I knew that Andrew and I weren't right for each other, but this breakup hit me hard—harder than any I'd ever had before. I think in many ways it was my first truly grown-up relationship. It was the first time I'd tried to really blend in with another person's life. And despite the fact that I was thinking of ending it myself, having him end it was awful. I was terribly unhappy with him, and yet I wasn't self-assured enough to listen to my own inner voice. For some reason, I hadn't had the strength to walk away, and that flattened me. How could he leave me, when I was supposed to be the one to leave him?

Meanwhile, I still ran into him at the gym all the time, which is enough to make anyone give up on exercise. I had always prided myself on being able to fall asleep the moment my head hit the pillow—it's a side effect of being constantly sleep deprived—but suddenly I couldn't sleep at night, and I was jittery and lost my appetite during the day because I was so upset. One night before I was supposed to do a live broadcast from Asbury Park I took a Benadryl (the poor man's Ambien) to help me sleep, and I ended up being so groggy the next day that I could barely string sentences together. Somehow I managed to pull it off. But no more Benadryl for me the night before a broadcast.

I wasn't just sad during this time, I was confused. On the one hand, I loved Andrew and I could imagine how nice it could be to make a life with him. On the other hand, I realized that I'd always felt on edge with him. Once our initial honeymoon period was over, I could never really be myself, I was always playing a part, like I was acting out lines in a play. I'd spent most of our relationship trying to prove myself to him and his family, and trying to prove that I was worthy. Now I knew that I needed to be true to myself in order to be happy, but I wasn't entirely sure what being true to myself meant.

ONE THING THAT I wasn't in conflict about during that time was having kids. Even when I was feeling deeply sad about Andrew, I never once woke up and thought, *Hurry up!* When I told my gynecologist that I'd just broken up with Andrew, she asked me if I wanted to freeze some eggs for a rainy day. There I was, in the most vulnerable position possible—knees splayed, feet in stirrups, cold instrument you know where—and I stared up at the ceiling feeling nothing. Other women in my situation might have cried. Other women had lain in that same position and been happy they were pregnant, or sad that they weren't, but they all *felt* something. I couldn't conjure a single emotion, though—all I could imagine were the feelings that other women might have. Meanwhile I was a completely blank slate.

So I said no to my gynecologist's question, just as simple as that, no more thought required. It might as well have been an SAT question that I knew by rote. It had never occurred to me to be worried about my fertility, or my ticking clock. Once I was out for drinks with a few friends and one told me about someone who'd just gotten married at age forty-two, and "Wasn't she lucky that it wasn't too late to have a family?" I didn't even know how to respond. My younger sister had always wanted kids—from the time we were little—and I'd always say, "You've got to be kidding me—coming from the family we did?" I don't know where she got her maternal instinct from, but clearly it wasn't passed on to me. Now I'm the first person to coo over a new baby, and I think children are incredibly precious and I really see how much joy they bring their parents. But I think my lack of emotion back then was a defense mechanism. I knew I wasn't ready for children and that I wouldn't have been a good parent at that point in my life, so I stopped myself from going there emotionally or even looking at my feelings about not having them.

I don't think every woman has to aim for marriage and kids, but I do think that the one downside for me in not aiming for those goals was that I kept looking for boyfriends instead of partners. I didn't have a picture of a life with a husband with whom you could share your innermost secrets. I had no idea that a husband could even fill that need. I had nothing to draw from in my upbringing. My aunt Nina had a happy marriage, but I wasn't around her and my uncle enough to understand how that could work in practical terms.

So I went back to dating for the sake of dating. My friend Susan and I were roommates in a Hamptons' share, and one night she said, "Let's do an experiment. We'll put on our most cleavage-baring tops and see how quickly it helps us meet guys." I was game, so I put on a low-cut black, stretchy, strappy top, and sure enough I met John. To this day, my friend and I laugh about the effectiveness of this strategy.

Maybe it wasn't actually the top, but John was definitely drawn to me, and I thought he was charming. He wasn't classically handsome, but he was tall and funny. We went to play tennis the next day, and we started dating. It wasn't sunbursts and star showers, but he made me laugh, and I was at a point in my life where I was starting to realize that no one was going to be a perfect amalgamation of everything I ever wanted.

I learned something in that relationship, though, and that is, there are things you should compromise on, and there are things that you shouldn't. Not too long after we started dating, cracks started to show in John's seemingly nice façade. He'd make little comments that weren't kind. A lot of times the cutting remarks related to money or my expensive taste.

I didn't need a man to be Daddy Warbucks, but I did want a man to be generous at heart. And I discovered that John had a really stingy side. It wasn't about how much money he spent, it was more about the feeling I got that he was always looking to cut corners, and that he was always aware of the price tag on everything. When he gave me a birthday present—an impersonal basket of generic bath and body products—I had the distinct impression that it was regifted. He presented me with a gold bracelet once, and despite the velvet box it came in, it had the look of something he'd bought from a shady guy off a table on Canal Street.

Then something awful occurred that ended up being a blessing in disguise. I was sleeping over at John's apartment when the phone rang. He answered it, and I could clearly hear a woman's voice on the other end, although I couldn't hear her words. John left the room and talked for a while and then he returned to bed later. I was suspicious, but I decided to file it away.

The next day I called him from work and I said, "So who called you in the middle of the night?" His response? "My buddy Dave." I'd met John's buddy Dave, and he was no boy soprano, so I said, "You're lying." Then I hung up the phone, and I never spoke to John again.

Maybe I still had some confusion when it came to long-term commitment and what that meant, but after Andrew and John it turns out that I'd developed some pretty clear lines in the sand when it came to an acceptable boyfriend:

1. He had to support my career.
2. He had to be generous.
3. He couldn't be a jerk.
4. He had to be truthful.
5. No cheaters allowed.

I was a lot less sad after John than I'd been after Andrew. John was like that bracelet he'd given me—shiny, brassy, weightless. And I knew I was worth a lot more than that.

These cookies are so sweet and delicious that if you're going through a breakup, you will soon forget about it. Or at least they will help ease the pain.

Traditional linzer hearts have little cutouts on the top so you can get a glimpse of the raspberry filling inside. You can make these linzer hearts the traditional way, but since I call them my "broken heart" cookies, I like cutting the hearts in half before I bake them (and in that case don't cut out the centers). When serving, arrange the cookies on a platter so that the halves aren't quite touching but you can still tell that they're hearts. Very cute.

LINZER BROKEN-HEART COOKIES

1½ cups almonds
3 tablespoons granulated sugar
1 cup confectioners' sugar, plus
  more for dusting
2¼ cups all-purpose flour
½ cup cornstarch
2¼ sticks unsalted butter, very
  cold
1 whole egg
1 egg yolk
6 ounces raspberry preserves
  (approximately)

Rolling pin
3-inch heart-shaped cookie
  cutter
1½-inch heart-shaped cookie
  cutter (optional, for cutting out
  the traditional way)
Cookie spatula
Parchment-lined cookie sheets
Mesh strainer

In a food processor (see note below), pulse almonds and granulated sugar until fine. Add confectioners' sugar, flour, and cornstarch, and pulse until well combined.

Cut cold butter into pieces and add to mixture in food processor.

Pulse until combined. Now add whole egg and egg yolk and pulse until mixture forms a smooth dough.

Divide dough into four disks and wrap each in plastic wrap. Refrigerate until firm (about 2 hours).

Preheat oven to 325 degrees.

On a flour-dusted surface, use a floured rolling pin to roll out each disk (one at a time) until ¼ inch thick.

If making broken-heart cookies, proceed to cut all the dough into 3-inch heart shapes, and then slice each heart in half using a very sharp knife. As you cut each half-heart, use your cookie spatula to transfer them to parchment-lined cookie sheets, spaced an inch apart.

If proceeding the traditional way, cut all the dough into 3-inch heart shapes, and then use a 1½-inch cutter to cut out the center of *half* of the 3-inch heart-shaped cookies. As above, use your cookie spatula to transfer the hearts to baking sheets as you go. Note that if you can't find a small heart-shaped cookie cutter, you can also use the base of a small rounded pastry tip. You can even cut out the centers with a sharp knife, if you have the patience for it.

After you cut out each batch of hearts (and heart-shaped centers), you'll have scraps left over. Gather them together, rechill if they've gotten soft, and continue to roll out as directed above.

Bake for 12 to 15 minutes, until pale golden in color. Do not overbake! Allow to cool on racks.

When cookies are cooled, set aside half the half-hearts, or all the whole hearts if you've made them the traditional way. Now flip over the remaining solid hearts or half-hearts and place ¾ teaspoon (or less, as needed) of preserves on each cookie bottom. Spread thinly, but not all the way to edges.

Put about ¼ cup of confectioners' sugar in a fine mesh strainer, and dust the tops of all the cookies that you set aside in the last step.

Place a dusted top onto a preserve-covered bottom and press lightly. Adorable, am I right?

Makes 32 hearts.

> *Note:* If you don't have a food processor, you can mix the first two ingredients in a blender and then proceed with the rest of the recipe using a standing mixer. In a pinch, you can use a hand mixer; it will just take you more time to incorporate the cold butter. If you don't have a blender, you can buy finely ground almonds and proceed the same way.

CHAPTER 14

IN CASE OF EMERGENCY, BREAK GLASS

It's easy not to focus on yourself and your problems when you're running so fast that you can't catch your breath. My years at Hot 97 were so insanely busy that I almost never took a pause to look at where my personal life was going and to really examine what I was doing wrong or right. Sure, I had my moments of clarity when a relationship ended, but they were just points on a graph. I hadn't connected the dots yet.

After Hot 97, I was offered a job to work on WOR's morning show. I had known about WOR AM radio since I was a kid, and the on-air personalities working there were New York institutions—Dr. Joy Browne, Joan Hamburg, and the Gambling family that had passed the baton of hosting *Rambling with Gambling* for generations. I had been working so long in the FM trenches, though, that I had to refresh myself where WOR AM was on the dial.

A live broadcast from Dublin, Ireland.

I was brought in to work with John Gambling, whose talk radio show went on at 5 A.M. (which meant I had to be at my desk by 4:30 at the latest). WOR wasn't looking for me to be a cohost with the kind of responsibility that I had at Hot 97, and I wouldn't be expected to attend station events every night. So despite the fact that I had to wake up at 3:10 A.M.—the earliest I'd ever had to get up for a job—I felt like I could take a deep breath for the first time in years (maybe ever). I stayed there for three years, and it's no coincidence that at a time when my work life became less frenetic, I started to really look inside and try to figure out what I needed to be happy.

When Andrew broke up with me, it really hit me that I hadn't been listening to myself—I had buried that little inner voice that tells you what feels right and what doesn't and replaced it with my imaginary ticker tape that just told me what I wanted to hear. I'd always avoided being terribly introspective. I found it too troubling. I preferred to just keep moving forward as opposed to looking back. And moving forward had the effect of drowning out that voice entirely. How can you listen to what's going on inside when you're working as hard as you can to make everything on the outside as noisy as possible? This is why people who work all the time are called workaholics. It's an addiction, and it was my self-medication of choice.

After my breakup with Andrew, I'd find myself crying out of nowhere when I was just walking down the street. I felt angry and disgusted when I broke up with John, but my response to Andrew was different. There was sadness, for sure, but my grief wasn't over the relationship itself. I was genuinely worried that I didn't know how to have a happy relationship and a happy life. I thought that all those people who'd managed to figure out the key to happiness must have been born with an internal compass that pointed them in roughly the right direction. Or maybe it was something instilled in them in childhood. Either way, I had no compass.

This wasn't depression. I didn't need a pill. I was at a crossroads, and I needed someone to give me the tools to fix my life and find the kind of happiness that can't be discovered on that next rung up the career ladder. I needed an expert, because left to my own devices I knew that I was going to keep flailing around in the dark and falling on my ass. At this point, I had no padding left back there.

I was so naive when I started therapy. I thought that I would walk in, tell the therapist my problems, and she'd fix them. It would be just like going to the chiropractor for a back adjustment. When that turned out to be a little pie in the sky, I thought that at minimum she'd give me a recipe for how I could fix myself—just follow these steps, bake for an hour, and voilà, you're done. But there was nothing easy and straightforward about therapy. It was absolutely horrible a lot of the time. I cried, I yelled. My therapist, Hettie, saw right through all my nonsense, and the experience of having her point out the truth behind my lifetime of denial was like having a full-body bandage ripped off over and over and over again. Hettie did not let me get away with *anything*.

I learned from Hettie that if you're not true to yourself, you become a bullshit artist. I had gotten very good at playing a shell game with myself and everyone else. I spun the cups around on the table, creating as many distractions as possible so that no one (myself included) ever knew where the truth lay. I convinced myself and everyone else that finding the right man was just a matter of time and luck. In truth, at the rate I was going I would never find a happy long-term relationship. I had no idea how to open myself up and to give at least as much as I got. I was a moving target with men, always on my toes, waving my arms in the air, distracting them with sex and cookies. And it wasn't just men I hid myself from—I never went very deep into my female friendships either. There was no one to whom I showed my insecurities or my vulnerable side. I buried that part of me underneath way too many layers of smoke and mirrors.

The problem with burying your personal truth so deeply—and under so much nonsense—is that you lose your sense of what you really want. Hettie pointed out to me that one of the reasons that I often felt taken advantage of in relationships—whether with men, or friends, or family, or even coworkers—is that I had no bottom line. I was so terrified of confrontation that I would run away rather than draw a line in the sand. She'd ask me, "Why not tell people what you want, what you will and won't accept? What are you so afraid of?"

I remember that I didn't even know how to answer that question. I guess it was obvious—after growing up in a household with so much angry conflict that it ended a marriage, I figured that all disagreement was bad and would result in disaster. So I just avoided conflict altogether, even if it meant bending over when I should have been standing firm, or running away from a perfectly good relationship when all it needed was a little fixing. When my parents were screaming and yelling at each other, I learned to shut up and not rock the boat. I never was taught the right way to be angry, and to express it. And what I learned as a kid I carried into adulthood. When I felt an uncomfortable emotion, I just stopped it up. When someone made me feel unworthy—whether it was a relative or a boyfriend or a girlfriend—I swallowed it. I didn't know that I could say "That hurts my feelings" or "Please don't do that" and that we could work things out and still be friends afterward. It was easier to run away, just like I'd always done.

Hettie could see the terror in my eyes at the mere thought of standing up for myself, so she suggested we role-play how I might handle conflict. She said, "Lisa, what's the worst thing that could happen if you stand up for yourself?"

I said, "Well, we'll get into a fight."

"What do you mean," Hettie said, "like a fist-fight?"

"No, like yelling and screaming, like my parents always did when they fought."

"Lisa, you don't have to yell to disagree with someone. You just tell them how you feel in a calm tone of voice. And then they tell you how they feel. Then you work things out and sometimes you compromise. Sometimes you say sorry and sometimes the other person does."

When she put it like that, I guess it made sense, but when you've lived your whole life believing that conflict is the end of the world, then it's very hard to start seeing it as a healthy part of life. So we started out slow, by pretending that she was a guy who hadn't called me back.

Hettie: Hey, Lisa, what's up?

Me: Well, I'm calling because I've been waiting to hear from you about our plans.

Hettie: Sorry about that, the time got away from me. How about I pick you up Friday at eight?

Me: When you tell me that you're going to call and then you don't, it makes me feel bad.

Hettie: I'm sorry, I'll give you more notice next time.

Of course it's a lot easier to say those things to your therapist than in a real-life situation, but over time I would incorporate what I learned in our role playing into my relationships. Once a coworker made a snotty comment to me. In the past I would have thought that I had to laugh it off and pretend it didn't bother me, even though it really hurt my feelings. But this time I called him on it. I said, "What do you mean by that?"

I still remember how that caught him up short, and how he was suddenly forced to explain himself. I walked away from that confrontation shaking my head in amazement. I actually thought to myself, *Oh my God, I'm still alive. No one died—the world didn't end. There was no screaming or yelling.* Who knew things could work that way? It was like a shade being lifted, and suddenly I didn't have to fumble around in the dark anymore.

Of course you don't change ingrained patterns overnight, and it wasn't like one positive experience with confrontation magically transformed me forever after. Revealing myself in that way continued to terrify me, and I didn't always practice what Hettie preached. As painful as it was to tamp down my emotions all the time and pretend they didn't exist, it was still a lot less scary than showing them. Telling people how you really feel requires a lot of bravery, and I had to admit that when it came to relationships, I was a big coward.

I was also a big liar a lot of the time. I didn't mean to be—or want to be—but I'd spent my whole life feeling like I had to be perfect and that any show of vulnerability was a massive failure. So I concealed any part of myself that might have seemed like a weakness. This meant that none of my relationships could be particularly close—even my friendships with people I loved, like Arlene. It took me a long time to learn that people actually feel more connected to you when they can help you in some way. Who can feel close to someone who is so guarded that he or she never admits to a less-than-happy emotion? All my friendships became much closer once I started to talk about my personality warts and shortcomings.

There was a downside to all this honesty, though.

When you experience true give-and-take with another human being, that's when you realize that you're really an adult. And that comes with a load of responsibility. I had to learn that honesty is a two-way street. If I could confront my friends and lovers, then that meant they could turn the tables right back on me.

When I told Hettie about the time that I'd turned down Michael's request that I walk in his charity walkathon, I expected her to sympathize with me, pat me on the head, and tell me that I was right not to let a man take advantage of me. Instead, she said that I was confusing selfishness with strength. She calmly pointed out that that's how I kept him and everyone else at arm's length. I made it clear to him that I was absolutely determined not to be Mrs. Traditional Somebody. But meanwhile I was expecting the guys I dated to be *Mr.* Traditional Somebody. My message to them was: have sex with me, take me out to dinner, but don't ask any deep questions, and don't ask too much of me, period.

On the one hand, I was deeply insecure—afraid that guys just wanted to date me for my sexy job and who I could introduce them to. On the other hand, I was subjecting men to the same superficial criteria. I wasn't interested in digging deep to find out their hopes and dreams, strengths and weaknesses. I probably would have been horrified if they'd tried to tell me any of that stuff. I was so used to staying on the surface in my relationships with men that even when I was with someone who deserved more from me and whom I really loved, I just . . . couldn't . . . do it. It felt a lot safer to sit on my fence, never committing to one side or the other. It would take a long time before I had the courage to stop my balancing act and make a decision to really commit and work at something.

Sometimes I think that all those hours I spent in therapy were actually harder than the years I spent doing the wrong things. It's sort of like the way diet and exercise are a lot harder than overeating. I'd been hiding beneath my layers of scar tissue and self-deception for years, and it wasn't an overnight process to unload it all. Often it would feel like one step forward and three steps back. A lot of times I felt worse walking out of Hettie's office than I had when I went in. It was like going in for a massage and getting beaten up instead. I couldn't believe I was paying good money to feel so terrible. But then one amazing day, I started to walk out feeling better.

Recently someone asked me if there was one moment during my time with Hettie when I discovered that I had it all figured out. But I don't think that's the way therapy works, even if it might feel that way sometimes. Instead, I think it's more like an archaeological dig. At first you're using a pickax and a shovel, pulling up rocks and boulders, and not really feeling like you're getting anywhere. Then you get down farther and you start chipping, chipping, chipping until you're gently peeling away the layers, finally dusting off the last bit of debris until something gorgeous emerges. It's a revelation, and it seems sudden, but it hasn't been sudden at all. It's been a lot of dirty, sweaty work.

Hettie was an amazing woman, and truly a godsend to me. That sentence is in the past tense because she passed away a few years back after battling MS. I still miss her, and after she died, I really wasn't sure I could go on without her. But then I looked inside myself and I discovered something amazing. She had left me with a treasure that she and I had uncovered together. After all those years of feeling lost in the woods, looking for some magical compass to show me the way, Hettie had taught me how to follow my own lead.

These cookies are so easy to make—unlike therapy, which took a lot of work and tears. They're also incredibly delicious—rich, moist, and fudgy on the inside, and with a thin layer of crispness on the outside. They are bumpy with chocolate chunks, which sort of reminds me of therapy—because I definitely hit a lot of bumps on the road to happiness. Really, I can't imagine my life without therapy or these cookies, so I think they are the perfect combination. Go to therapy, have some of these after. Or make these for a friend (or boyfriend) who could use a little sweet therapy themselves.

CHOCOLATE THERAPY CHUNK COOKIES

2⅔ cups semisweet chocolate
   chips, divided
¼ cup (½ stick) unsalted butter
¾ cup packed brown sugar
2 eggs
1 teaspoon vanilla

½ cup flour
¼ teaspoon baking powder
1½ cups semisweet chocolate
   chunks

Parchment-lined cookie sheets

Preheat oven to 350 degrees.

Microwave semisweet chips on high for 1 to 2 minutes. Stir chocolate until smooth.

In a separate bowl, mix butter and sugar until fluffy. Add eggs and vanilla until incorporated well. Pour in melted chocolate. Make sure to scrape down the sides of the bowl.

In a small bowl, combine flour and baking powder. Add to chocolate mixture and mix well. Now fold in remaining chips and chocolate chunks.

Using a small ice cream scoop, place scoops of dough on parchment-lined cookie sheets, 1 inch apart. Bake 12 to 13 minutes. Cookies will puff up a bit and look set when done. As with almost all cookies (especially chocolate), it's better to err on the side of caution and pull them out sooner rather than later.

Cool on cookie sheet for about a minute, then transfer to rack to cool completely.

Makes 60 small cookies.

CHAPTER 15

LATE BLOOMER

My biggest life epiphany came at the oddest moment. It wasn't a dramatic scene. Nothing extraordinary happened. But the moment hit me like an avalanche and made me rethink once and for all what I was looking for in life.

I was casually dating someone much younger than me. Tyler was a nice guy, but not someone I was having deep, meaningful conversations with. And he was not the kind of guy I should have been spending time and energy on anymore—definitely not after all the therapy I'd been going to. I should have known better, and I suppose I did, but getting a concept intellectually and really internalizing it are two different things. It should have been obvious to me that a young, fancy-free guy was not a marker on the road to happiness for me at that point in life. But no one could have convinced me of that—not my friends, and not even Hettie. I think on some level I believed that if I dated this young, silly guy, then that meant I was still young and silly, too.

One night Tyler invited me to a party at his apartment. So I went, even though I really didn't know anyone and it was definitely not my scene. It got late, the apartment was stiflingly crowded, and it became crushingly obvious to me that I had zero in common with anyone there—including Tyler. Finally, I thought to myself, *What am I doing here? He's not even my boyfriend. Why am I wasting my time?*

That was not my big epiphany, though. What really smacked me in the face occurred a few minutes later when I walked out of Tyler's building onto the dark city street. As I stepped off the curb to hail a cab, I saw an SUV pull up in front of a nearby building. Out of the car stepped a man around my age—I don't even really remember what he looked like. Nothing about him was exceptional; he was just an average-looking adult male. He opened the passenger door and his wife emerged. Then he opened the back door of the car, reached in, and after a moment I saw that he had pulled a baby out of a car seat.

Wham. There it was.

No, I did not suddenly hear wedding bells tinkling in my ears. Nor did my ovaries instantly explode with longing to have a child. That was not what the universe was telling me in that moment. Instead, the message I got that night was something much simpler: what I really wanted was to be a responsible adult—someone who loved and cared for myself as well as others. Someone who had responsibilities to people outside of work. Someone on whom other people relied, and who had people to rely on when I needed them, too. Because that's what an adult is.

That's when everything finally clicked into place—the years of crying in Hettie's office, the momentary flashes of insight when I ended it with one guy and decided what I was looking for in another. Click, click, click.

I had just grown up. Congratulations, Lisa, you win a cookie.

IT'S KIND OF EMBARRASSING to be such a late bloomer. Shouldn't I have felt like an adult at least twenty years before? But I guess it would be worse to be one of those people who thinks she has it all figured out at age twenty-two, at which point there's nowhere to go but down. So I choose to look at it optimistically—I am definitely one of those people who learns something new every day.

Of course I still had my ups and downs in romance after that. It's not like I decided one day that I was going to grow the hell up and then poof, Prince Charming walked through the door and I was ready to embrace him with open arms. And it's not as if

I immediately, miraculously struck the ideal balance between work and personal life. I had some tough times adjusting to this new version of myself.

My first attempt at putting aside foolish things was really not so auspicious.

I met Gavin at a college reunion. Enough said, right? I should just stop right there. But I was trying to be different, and not to judge men based on flimsy assumptions. I decided to be open to second chances and second meetings. He was a really nice guy, a hard worker, and a great conversationalist. There was just one problem: he kissed like a snake. This is no exaggeration. He had this sharp little tongue and it would dart into my mouth, and it simultaneously freaked me out and nauseated me. It was so pointy that I didn't know if he was kissing me or flossing my teeth.

Despite this, I kept trying to make it work with Gavin—I couldn't believe that I was going to break up with a guy over something so seemingly trivial. So I kept trying, and I even gave Gavin subtle lessons. "Hey, babe, how about we try it this way . . . I'll put my tongue in your mouth, but you just relax yours . . . relax. No, relax. Um, could you try relaxing your tongue?" Nothing worked. His tongue was absolutely impervious to instruction, and when he kissed me, I felt like I had a floundering goldfish trapped in my mouth. No matter how hard I tried not to be disgusted, I wanted to hurl. Finally, I was so distraught that I actually prayed at the end of my bed. I'd never been to a mass in my life, but I got on my knees like a Catholic schoolgirl and I begged God to teach me how to love this guy.

My prayers were not answered, and finally I decided that a mature adult does not lead a man on this way. If I couldn't kiss Gavin, then I couldn't love him, and therefore I needed to break up with him. So I did. I was really upset about it though, and I confessed the whole thing to a girlfriend, certain that she would tell me that I was a terrible person for ending it with Gavin. Instead, she told me that she once had a boyfriend who kissed like a cow (big, thick tongue), and she broke up with him, too. Then another friend told me she broke up with a guy who kissed like a hairy bison. Every time he kissed her she'd have long red scratches on her face from his coarse soul patch. I was very relieved to hear that I was not alone in dating a man who kissed like the resident of a petting zoo. Old MacDonald had a farm, ee i ee i . . . eew!

I WAS STILL WORKING at WOR when my producer walked over to my desk and said he had an e-mail for me that had come into the morning show's general address. Normally listeners who wanted to reach me directly e-mailed me through my website, so this was unusual. And it also wasn't private—now multiple people had read this e-mail before it ever even reached me.

The e-mail was from a guy named Adam. His mother listened to WOR in the morning. Something about my personality, she told her son, convinced her that he and I would be a good match. So she urged him to write to me.

This all might sound a little stalkerish if it weren't for the fact that it was one of the sincerest, most thoughtful e-mails I'd ever received. Adam was also open and up-front about his intentions. "I'm a normal guy from Long Island," he wrote. "Why not take a chance?"

Why not? That was a really good question. I was trying to open up more, right? Here was a person who seemed like a genuinely nice guy, who simply wanted to meet me and see if we hit it off. So what was the harm? Before I jumped at the bait though, I wanted to make sure that I wasn't completely losing my mind. The staff at WOR was very much like a family, and since everyone knew about this e-mail already, I decided to show it to my coworker Mara to make sure she didn't spot any latent serial-killer tendencies. She was single and had spent enough time on JDate to be able to read between the lines. She read the e-mail and thought it was sweet too. Meanwhile, everyone else at the station seemed sincerely happy that I might actually meet a listener who'd written to me.

And okay, I should also add that in the e-mail Adam included a photo, and I couldn't help noticing that he was handsome and had great, sparkling eyes.

So I decided to call him, and we hit it off right away. He was recently divorced and he had a young child. Instead of running for the hills like I might have done before, I thought, *Great.* Hadn't I wanted to be with a real adult with adult responsibilities?

Adam and I met for a drink soon after our first phone call. Those sparkling eyes weren't just a photographic trick, because he still had them. He also had a great smile and thick, dark hair, which I liked.

On our first date, Adam looked at me like I was Angelina Jolie. And just like his e-mail, his attention to me seemed utterly sincere. I didn't think I'd ever been with a man who made me feel so fully appreciated, like he felt lucky to be with me. Maybe some of the men I'd been with over the years really did feel that way—and maybe they even showed it. But either I had been oblivious or I had been so terrified of intimacy that I had purposely looked the other way. As Adam looked at me with stars in his eyes, I felt complimented and unsettled all at the same time. But I forced myself to stay open to whatever might happen with him.

Still, there were a few things about Adam that concerned me. He had been divorced only for a few months. He'd also recently moved into his mom's finished basement. That last part wasn't a deal breaker—he was in transition and I knew he'd eventually get his own place. But the first part was troubling. It didn't bother me that he was a dad. I felt like enough of an adult at that point to at least consider having a relationship with a man who had a child. No, what worried me was the recent divorce. I'd always heard you shouldn't date a man until he's been out of his marriage for at least a year. For God's sake, I was even working with radio relationship expert Dr. Joy Browne, and her mantra was . . . *Don't get involved with a recently divorced man!* I didn't want to ignore my standards—or my smarts—with Adam, but I had also come to realize that there is no such thing as Mr. Perfect. The bottom line was that Adam was a good man, and he seemed worth taking a chance on.

Because I really liked Adam, I didn't want to jump into bed with him right away. I wanted us to get to know each other first, take our time. I'd suddenly gone from a *Sex and the City* character to a Jane Austen character. Not that things were boring. We went on a lot of fun dates, and he loved city nightlife. So he was always eager to come in for whatever events I was invited to. I hadn't always been comfortable including men in that part of my life, but I was very pleasantly surprised when Adam showed up at one of our first big evenings together dressed really sharp, right down to his choice of denim. He might have been a dad, but he didn't wear dad jeans, thank God. And Adam didn't just fit in visually, he was also charming and could talk to anyone. It was amazing for me to be with someone who could blend so seamlessly with my life, without wanting all the spotlight for himself the way some of the other guys I'd dated had—this was definitely a first for me.

Once the weather got nicer, Adam invited me out to his mother's home (I brought my chocolate chip cheesecake bars, always an easy hit). Adam's mom was so excited to meet me. Not only did she feel partly responsible for our meeting, but she seemed thrilled that her son was happy again. When we arrived, she was preparing dinner and the house smelled delicious. Our first course would be chicken soup, and when I went in the kitchen to offer her some help, she pulled me aside and said, "You'll have to learn how to make this. Adam loves it." I think I gulped. I hadn't even slept with the guy yet—it felt a little premature to start learning family recipes.

Coincidentally, our physical relationship was just about to steam up. The days were getting longer and the weather was warm, so Adam and I decided to take a walk around his neighborhood before dinner. We took a stroll past the local elementary school that looked a lot like the one I attended. A single-level building with a big playground with swings, a jungle gym, and picnic tables. Such a sweet, innocent scene—that was just about to be violated by our raging hormones.

Adam and I settled at one of the picnic tables and before you know it, we started making out. Soon we were actually lying on top of the table. It was getting dark, but it wasn't *that* dark and there were plenty of streetlights, so I kept one eye peeled for anyone who might see us. At one point I sat up and tried to bring some sanity to the proceedings. "What are we doing? Kids eat lunch where our asses are right now!" But then Adam started kissing me again and I stopped caring. Adam definitely knew what he was doing, and it was exciting to let loose a little bit. There's nothing like doing something forbidden in a public place to get your juices flowing. The risk that an unsuspecting dog walker—or God forbid, the cops—might walk by just added to the thrill.

After twenty minutes or so, we called a time-out and fixed ourselves up as best we could. I checked my jeans for pizza and chocolate milk stains, felt for splinters in my butt, and then we walked back to his mom's house for dinner. In a bit of surreal timing, that was when I met Adam's daughter for the first time. She was too young to put two and two together and realize that I was dating her dad. This took the pressure off things—I could just be a nice lady, instead of some scary specter of a stepmother. Truth be told, that would have been a frightening prospect to me, too. I was just learning how to take care of myself, much less taking on that kind of responsibility. Maybe eventually I would be ready to embrace it, but not quite yet.

Adam and I finally had sex the night of my cookie party. This was going to be one of my biggest bashes ever—celebrity chefs, press, a huge invite list—and I was eager to show off Adam. I was also excited to show Adam my new outfit—a black sequined top and tight satin jeans. Some couples might have discussed when they were going to have sex the first time, but I didn't tell Adam that I'd already decided that was the night. So when I basically ripped his clothes off after the last guest left, he was a little surprised. He got over the shock quickly, and I learned that our picnic bench wrestling match was just the prelude to the main event. Dr. Joy Browne may be right that you shouldn't date a recently divorced man, but you should definitely date a man who's already spent years perfecting his craft.

Everything was going well with Adam. We seemed to be bending our lives to meet in the middle, just the way I thought you were supposed to do in a healthy, adult relationship.

Then I made a mistake. Or maybe it wasn't my mistake—maybe it was his. Either way, I said something that drove him away. It happened one Sunday morning when he was leaving my apartment to go to a football game. I was still in bed and I whispered, "I'll miss you." I didn't give the words a second thought, they just came out of me, as sincere and honest as his first e-mail to me had been.

He didn't call that evening after the game, as he normally would. And suddenly, instead of being up for anything and always available, he was "too busy at work" to see me. I knew the sound of an excuse when I heard one—I'd made too many of them myself not to recognize the signs of someone pulling away.

Finally, we got together for "the talk." He told me that he really cared about me, but that he "wanted to be friends." The excuse he gave was that he needed to concentrate on his work.

He wanted to be friends? But we weren't friends. We were way more than that. I knew in my gut, in an instant, that being friends with him wouldn't be good for me. I had plenty of friends already—really good friends who loved me—and I didn't need an ex-boyfriend to fill the friend stable. I'd only get mixed signals from him, I'd end up feeling bad, and I'd certainly end up hurt far worse than I was already. So, without thinking much more than a second, I said, "No. Either we're a couple or we're not."

I knew it was the right thing to say, but still, I couldn't believe those words came out of my mouth. They came from inner strength and self-esteem. These were things with which I didn't have a whole lot of familiarity.

Adam teared up, and I cried too. It was very sad. I think I cried an entire week after that. I had some moments of doubt that made the whole thing feel even worse. I kept questioning myself—had I made the right decision? Other women have remained friends with exes and end up getting back together and eventually marrying, why not us? I also felt the pain of letting go of someone I really cared about. But as confused as I often felt, I always came back to my gut certainty that I'd made the right choice for me—and probably for him as well.

We're often told to stand our ground and fight, to never give up. But sometimes it's harder to walk away from a difficult situation than it is to stay and keep struggling. It would have been easier to relent to Adam, and keep a glimmer of hope that he'd change his mind. But in the end, that would have been a disaster and I knew it. I'd rather experience some up-front misery than to sign on to a long, hopeless slog. Pre-epiphany, I would have chosen the slog, but now I didn't even consider it. I had officially bloomed—and better late than never.

I may have soured on romance at various points, but somehow I always came back around to seeing how sweet life can be. So I

came up with a recipe for this chapter that's a perfect combination of sour and sweet. These aren't your typical lemon bars, which can be mouth-puckering and adults-only. Even kids (and those clinging to childhood) love my lemon bars, because they taste just like ice cream. (PS, they're also really good à la mode.)

LEMONS-INTO-LEMONADE BARS

1 cup (2 sticks) butter, at room
   temperature
1 cup sugar
2 cups flour
1¼ cup oatmeal (not instant)

Juice of 3 lemons
Grated zest of 2 lemons
1 (14-ounce) can sweetened
   condensed milk

Preheat oven to 350 degrees.

Line a 9 x 13–inch pan with parchment paper so the sides overhang.

Cream butter and sugar until fluffy. Add flour, then the oatmeal. Set aside.

In a separate bowl, stir juice and zest into milk until well incorporated.

Press two-thirds of the dough into the pan. Now spread the lemon-milk mixture over dough. Break up and distribute the remaining dough over the top, so it resembles a streusel.

Bake 30 to 35 minutes, until topping turns golden.

Cool completely, then slice. Keep refrigerated in an airtight container.

Makes about 32 squares, depending on how small you cut them.

CHAPTER 16

GETTING LUCKY

I don't get lonely. Despite the fact that I can be the life of the party, and for years I threw myself into every major launch, promotional event, and concert I was invited to, I've actually never been afraid to be alone. The downside of this is that I have never felt like I needed a partner to make me feel complete. The upside of this is that I have never felt like I needed a partner to make me feel complete. On the one hand, it's made me less likely to reach out, but on the other hand, it's given me high standards. After Adam and I broke up, I realized that I was doing just fine on my own. It's not that I wouldn't have been happy to meet someone wonderful, but only if he were truly right for me—and good for me. I didn't need to be with someone because I was afraid not to have a boyfriend on Saturday night.

I had definitely come to appreciate my close friendships over the years. The less I stopped spinning like a manic top, the more I noticed how lovely it could be just to hang out with a girlfriend or two and talk. I still had fun and could enjoy a great party, but it didn't have to be every night. Being alone with myself was really nice, too.

Once I broke free of my old ways in my personal life, I made a change in my work life as well. I'd been at WOR for three years when I realized that I wanted a different kind of challenge. I'd been walking a straight line of job to job to job, and I suddenly felt a strong desire to branch out, and to do something for me. I had a website before a lot of celebrities (and companies) even thought of that, and I'd always been really smart about marketing myself—after all, I'd pretty much single-handedly gotten myself on TV. So I decided to leave WOR and start my own marketing and public relations business, working for myself for the first time in my life. The thought of giving up a steady paycheck was terrifying, but I reminded myself that I'd turned a little friends-only cookie party into an annual, star-studded bash. I had corporate contacts, and I'd been promoting a product—myself—for years, and doing a really good job at it.

I knew that there was a time limit to how long I could rest on my radio laurels, and I needed to pick up some clients before people thought I was old news.

There were only so many months that I could introduce myself as Lisa G., formerly of Hot 97, WOR,
and so on. So I went to a million events, networked
and called people until my fingers bled, and I got
clients right away. Self-confidence is contagious, I
learned—if you have enough faith in yourself, other
people have faith in you too.

I specialized in web marketing, which was still
in its very early days, and it turned out that even big
companies with huge marketing departments needed
the expertise of people like me. Nike hired me after I
handed out cards at the Rucker Park basketball tour-
nament in Harlem, and Purina hired me to host and
produce videos for their "Greatest American Dog
Challenge," which was kind of an Olympics for dogs,
only instead of discus throwing, there was Frisbee
catching.

It was around this time, when I had all this
newfound flexibility in my schedule, that I decided
to pick up the violin again. You probably forgot all
about how I played the violin, didn't you? Well, I
hadn't forgotten, and I'd always longed for it. I was
terrified that if I picked it up again I'd find out that
I'd lost any talent or skill I once had, but I put aside
my fear and decided that I needed and wanted the
violin in my life.

I looked up a place called Strings and Other
Things, on the Upper West Side, and I rented myself
a violin. Then I registered for a basic violin class at the

New School. Back in college I was way, way beyond basic violin, but I truly didn't know now if my skill would come back to me. I figured that if I took the beginner class, I could just start from scratch when I inevitably fell flat on my face.

Even though I had the violin before I went to class the first time, I refused to touch it—I wouldn't even take it out of the case. I was too afraid to pick up the bow and find out how bad I was. I figured I would delay the heartbreak of learning that I'd lost it. The night of my first class I was terrified, but within three minutes of starting the class, lo and behold, it had all come back to me. It was like riding a bicycle. Actually, it was more like skiing. I still had all the moves I'd had as a kid, but now I had something new and adult: trepidation. The same way kids don't worry about breaking a leg on the slope but adults do, I now felt an unfamiliar fear of making too great a leap on the violin, challenging myself too much, shifting up to third position and taking those notes quite as fast as I once did. But that fear was something I could live with—and get past—as long as I could at least play.

The New School's music program at night was a hilarious, freewheeling place. There were all kinds of classes going on all the time. Mine was the only group violin class, so while we played our refined chamber music, in every other room there were all kinds of guitar lessons, and rock and jazz bands.

There were all these people having fun all the time, and every once in a while when my quiet little group was on a break I'd peek in on one of the other classes to see what they were up to. I remember one particular band had a Wall Street banker-looking guy on guitar and a Hasidic Jew—payos and all—on drums. The musicians came in all shapes and sizes, all exercising their secret passions. And here I thought I was the only one.

At the end of the semester I realized that I needed more of a musical challenge than the beginner class. I actually tried private lessons for a short while, but I found that I missed the musical camaraderie of a group. This was really different for me—to feel that I wanted other people to share my experience with. Chamber music is so much about teamwork and interdependence. The fact that I craved it and enjoyed it so much was a really big step for me—or a rediscovery, more accurately. I'd loved this aspect of music when I was younger, but over the years of depending just on myself and keeping my eyes on the prize, I had lost touch with how wonderful it was to lift instruments together.

Eventually, when it was time to renew my violin rental, I decided to go ahead and purchase my violin. This was major. I would say that it was like buying a car, but it was more serious than that because a violin you have for a lifetime and the average Toyota you do not. When I paid for it, the store employees gathered around me to say congratulations and shake my hand. You'd think I was getting bat mitzvahed. Or married. Which, in a way, I was. Because this was also about love and commitment, and I'd shown that I had both.

FROM WORKING FOR MYSELF to playing the violin again, this was a year of awakening for me. So far, all my risk taking had paid off, so I was probably ripe for the plucking when a casual acquaintance of mine said that she thought I should mentor high school students. She didn't know me well at all, so I'm not sure what she saw in me that day to make her think that I could do it. Maybe I had a searching look on my face. Whatever her reason, she said she thought I'd enjoy it, and instantly, it felt to me like the right thing to do. She was a math teacher at LaGuardia, the highly regarded Manhattan arts high school (also known as the school from *Fame*), and she said that she'd sponsor me to be a mentor in their program.

I passed the background check (ha!) and was invited to an orientation in which the prospective mentors were given all the ground rules—where we could take the kids, and what our exact responsibilities and time commitment would be. They made it very clear that meetings were to occur weekly, and that if we didn't intend to stick with our student throughout their high school career, then we shouldn't do it. I gulped and signed on.

Over the course of my time there, I would sponsor two students—both remarkable girls—and I would become deeply attached to both of them. I'd chat with the girls, listen to their boyfriend sagas, give them judicious yet nonjudgmental advice when I thought they needed it. It was unlike any volunteer work I'd ever done before. In radio we were always doing big events for charities, and truthfully it was just like another day at the station. There was no getting your hands dirty, no real interaction with the people that you were supposedly helping. And those charity events were usually once-a-year gigs—no one expected me to keep a hand in. There was no one with a name and a life story that I knew, who would depend on me to be there and not flake out, who looked up to me as a role model.

I'll never forget my first day picking up Olivia, the first student I worked with. I waited for her outside the school, and a group of teenagers were goofing around. One of them started pelting me with jelly beans, and I thought to myself: *What the heck am I doing here? I don't belong here.* At that moment, all I wanted to do was pick up those jelly beans from the ground and throw them right back at the brat. But I suspected that wasn't in the LaGuardia guidelines for mentors. I felt like such a fish out of water, and I was full of self-doubt. What was I going to say to this teenaged girl? What did I possibly have to offer her?

Finally I found Olivia and we went someplace nearby to have coffee. Very quickly I realized that she wasn't looking for a teacher or a parent or even an authority figure—she already had those in her life. She needed a friend, and one with a little sense and perspective. Most of the kids who signed up for the mentoring program (or were forced to sign up by their parents) were feeling a little lost, a little outcast. But because they all went to LaGuardia, they were also passionate about the arts—they were talented and focused, but also incredibly confused. It was like seeing myself in a mirror—they all knew *what* they desperately wanted to be, they just weren't at all sure who they really were.

The thing I learned most from that experience was that ultimately I got way more out of my relationship with those girls than they got from me. I did help them—I was there for them rain or shine for years, and I made calls, got them internships, that kind of thing. Olivia's mom said she thought I had saved her daughter's life at a time when she might have spiraled downward. That meant the world to me, but as wonderful as my girls were, I bet they would have found their way without me. I'm not so sure that I would have done the same thing without them, though—the inspiration that I got from those girls, and the newfound respect I gained for my own ability to give to someone else, was life changing for me.

I'M A CREATURE OF habit, and years of radio have taught me one of my most die-hard mantras: *On time is late.* In radio, you always want to be early. So very often when I was going to my weekly violin class, I was quite early and I had time to kill in the neighborhood. Pretty frequently I would be drawn to the same pet store and its display of kittens. I'd stare at them, enjoy watching them play, and track their growth from week to week. I'd never wanted a pet before, but suddenly I was obsessed.

Which didn't mean that I actually wanted a cat for myself. No way. I just liked looking at them . . . right?

Pretty soon, my kitten obsession became a running joke with my friends, who wondered why I didn't just take the plunge and get one. I mean, it was obvious that I wanted one—why else would I be looking at them so much? But I had every excuse not to get one. This one was sick, I said, this one wasn't orange enough. That one didn't have enough stripes, that one was too big or too black. I came up with a million bizarre and contradictory standards for what would make the perfect kitten for me. And there were just so many kittens to choose from! I got overwhelmed at the number, and the thought of making a decision, so I just didn't make one at all.

By this point I had gotten to know the owners of the pet store, and they pointed out a new litter of kittens to me and told me the sad story of how someone had left the pregnant mother for dead outside their door. They took her in, slowly nursed her back to health, and now they had these kittens to find homes for. The runt of the litter was a tiny little tabby, and he became my focus over the coming weeks. There were lots of other kittens around—healthy, happy, playful kittens that had a lot better chance of survival than my malnourished little runt. But those other kittens didn't do it for me. I looked forward to seeing my little guy—maybe I saw a little bit of myself in this scrappy, disfavored child. Every week I'd ask after his health, and every week he got a little bigger. Finally, I said the words: "I'll take him."

I couldn't take him home until he was eight weeks old, but once I decided he'd be mine, there was no going back, no changing my mind. I'd made a commitment, just like I'd recommitted myself to the violin and devoted myself to my LaGuardia girls.

The day I took my kitten home, the pet store gave me a carrying case fit for a full-sized animal, so big for this tiny little creature that you could barely see in there. He was eight weeks old, but closer to the size and strength of a five-week-old—he seemed so fragile and breakable, with a heart the size of a hummingbird's. I think the pet store owners could see the panic in my eyes and realized I had no idea what the heck I was doing. So they also loaded me up with a litter pail, a scoop, and some food. Then they sent me on my way—no doubt with their fingers crossed behind their backs. Riding home on the subway, strangers looked into the carrying case quizzically, trying to figure out what that little ball of fur in there might be. One person actually said, "Is it a rat?"

Meanwhile, the whole way home I was crying and thinking to myself, *What am I doing? He's going to die—I'm going to kill him.* I didn't know how to take care of anything, not really—I didn't even have plants. All I had to guide me in how to keep this little ball of fur alive was a cat book. So I made an appointment with a vet the next day, and I prayed to the universe that my runt didn't die in the night.

He didn't. And twelve years later he still hasn't. After he'd been with me about a week, I told my eight-year-old niece that she could name my new kitten. She instantly came up with the name Lucky. Her attraction to that name wasn't poetic—she happened to really like that brand of jeans. But my love for the name was a little deeper. He deserved that name, I knew, because every step of the way he could have not made it. He was a little survivor, and he was definitely lucky. And over time, I'd come to realize just how lucky I was to have him.

First, though, I had to get used to the demon that I had unleashed in my home. Every night at 1 A.M. he would jump all over the apartment—maybe I should have known, but no one told me that cats were naturally nocturnal. And kittens are insane. So there I was—the woman who'd never sought out heavy responsibilities in my personal life, who'd never had a single maternal yearning—and I had a living thing in my house who literally cried for my attention in the middle of the night. What had I done? Lucky didn't even look like a domesticated cat. He's got these huge eyes and this long, pink nose. I briefly wondered if the pet store had sent me home with an ocelot.

I would like to say that I fell in love with Lucky right away, but no. Despite the multiple wake-ups every night, he was a sweet, lovable little thing, introducing himself—and charming—every human who walked through the door. But at first I wouldn't open up to him. Whether from fear or from long-held routine, I just couldn't accept that there was a living thing in my home that it was my responsibility to love. So every morning when I went to work, I didn't lavish him with attention before I left. I'd kind of nod at him and say, "Okay, cat, here's your food, here's your water, have a nice day." I changed his litter box regularly and I spent hundreds of dollars on vet bills. I was doing all the things that a responsible pet owner should do. But the love part? That took some time.

Then one day, I noticed that Lucky couldn't open one of his eyes. So I took him to the vet, who told me that Lucky had scratched a cornea. They could perform a procedure to fix it and he'd be as good as new, but they would need to keep him overnight. I would have to leave him there. Alone. In a cage.

That's when I started to sob.

You would think that poor little Lucky was having open heart surgery, the way I was carrying on. All I could think about was how much he needed me, and how I'd nursed him to health, and how I couldn't possibly lose him now—I couldn't bear it. And there it was rising up inside of me: love. Lucky needed me, and I needed him.

Lucky's cornea healed, and I eventually stopped sobbing. Flash forward about a year, and I noticed that Lucky was having these strange, spastic back spasms that looked like rapid ripples down his back. It frightened me, so I took him to the vet. My usual vet was on vacation, and the associate on call was Dr. Lawrence Putter, who would eventually become a dear friend of mine. He examined Lucky and said, "You know, I think this is something I read about in medical school—a rare kind of epilepsy." Sure enough, one ridiculously expensive veterinary neurology visit later, it turned out that Dr. Putter was right. And now I am the proud owner of a cat that I adore who requires two doses of phenobarbital every day. Every single day. Which means that if I want to go away, I hire a cat sitter to give him his medicine twice a day. Yes, I have a cat nanny. And do I mind? Not at all.

I get teased now about being a cat lady, like I'm this pathologically animal-attached person who loves cats more than people. If those teasers only knew what a huge thing it was for me just to keep a cat alive—much less to love him as much as I do—they might think differently. But when they kid me that way, I just laugh along. I figure I'm not a cat lady— I'm a lucky lady.

Not too many people make biscotti at home. I think that's because they assume that they're going to be really hard to make, or that they won't turn out well. Fear keeps us from taking chances, as I have learned more than once. And just like Lucky ended up being a risk worth taking for me, these biscotti are totally rewarding to make—and incredibly easy. You'll make them, love them, and wonder why you waited so long. Like so many things in life.

CHOCOLATE CHIP BISCOTTI

2 cups all-purpose flour

1 cup sugar

1 teaspoon baking powder

¼ teaspoon cinnamon

4 tablespoons cold butter

3 large eggs lightly beaten
   (reserving 1 tablespoon)

1 teaspoon vanilla extract

1 cup semisweet chocolate chips

Decorative large sugar crystals
   (optional)

Parchment-lined cookie sheets

Pastry brush

Serrated knife

Preheat oven to 350 degrees.

Mix flour, sugar, baking powder, and cinnamon in large bowl. Cut in butter with two knives or a pastry blender until mixture looks like small crumbs.

Add beaten egg (minus reserved tablespoon) and vanilla. Stir until a moist dough forms. Stir in chocolate chips.

Divide dough into quarters. With floured hands, shape each quarter into a 9 x 2–inch log. Place the logs on parchment-lined cookie sheets. If baking two logs per sheet, be sure to place the logs at least 4 inches apart since the logs will spread as they bake.

With a pastry brush, brush the top of each log with reserved egg. If you like, sprinkle with large sugar crystals.

Bake 25 minutes. Cool for 10 minutes.

Place one log at a time on cutting board. With serrated knife, cut warm log crossways into ½-inch diagonal slices. Place slices upright on cookie sheets. Repeat process with remaining logs.

Bake 15 minutes, until biscotti turn just slightly golden.

Cool on wire racks.

Makes 5 dozen.

CHAPTER 17

PERFECT IS BORING

After a few happy years of having my own company, I got a call to return to radio. The offer was to work on the *Howard Stern Show* on SiriusXM—really the Holy Grail of radio and the kind of opportunity you don't even dare to fantasize about. Howard was creating a news department—he came up with the idea in the shower—and my radio rabbi, Walter Sabo (who was a consultant for the channel), recommended me. I went in and visited the station, and it felt like I'd walked into radio heaven. I was surrounded by people I'd always admired—it was like being recruited to play for the Yankees. I couldn't believe so much talent was in one place. Over the years I've spent there I've had the opportunity to work with broadcasting pros like Gary Dell'Abate, Tim Sabean, Liz Aiello, and Brad Driver. Most of all, of course, there's Howard himself. Working for him has made me fall in love with radio all over again. His show combines everything I've ever loved about radio—it's challenging, a load of work, and full of people who make me laugh every day of my life. I feel so fortunate.

Because I respect Howard so much, from the start I felt a huge responsibility to do a great job and to always bring back amazing red-carpet audio from awards shows to use on our show. This was not easy. Despite the fact that Howard's listeners were in the millions and some TV shows only had viewers in the tens of thousands (if that), having a camera gave the TV people pride of place on the red carpet, which then gave them the best access to the celebrities as they exited their limos. In addition, our news department was new and many publicists didn't understand or know that we were a legitimate news team. Meanwhile, I was stuck way back in nowheresville, crammed against a metal police barrier. I'd be screaming my lungs out with my little digital recorder and trying to get the celebrities to notice me before their publicists shoved them into the event that they were already late for. To add further insult, I was actually given a worse position than reporters from every single website, no matter how rinky-dink. People representing websites with hits in the double digits were getting better access to celebrities than I was, representing the *Howard Stern Show*. When I covered one awards show, the cable network actually stuck me outside in the cold, while other reporters got to stand inside in a heated red carpet tent. Not only did I freeze my butt off, but I got zero audio, and there wasn't a thing I could do about it. Here's my view from outside the tent:

 The network apologized for my placement and the apology was accepted. But still, I constantly had to contend with being shoved to the back of the red carpet. Often, by the time the celebrity got to the end of the carpet, the publicist would say to me—and the handful of reporters from never-heard-of-it dot-coms that I was stuck there with—that we'd have to do a group interview. This meant that they expected us to pull together in a pathetic scrum and all ask the same question and use the same audio. This drove me crazy, and I'd turn into a possessed loudmouth, for which I do not apologize. It was my job to get great audio, and I was not going to fail in that task. So I just pretended those other guys weren't there, and I shoved my way to the front and asked my questions.

Aside from my lousy placement, the problem was that at five foot three in a chaotic crush like that, I was practically invisible and my screams and wails were not getting me the interviews I needed. I was crowded out by camera people who had to stand behind the barrier with me, and I was blocked by the on-camera reporters who actually got to stand in front of the barrier (do not even get me started on the unfairness of that). So I rigged a sign like the ones that limo drivers use at airports that said "Howard Stern" in capital letters, and when I held that up and added it to my screaming, I started to get more celebrities to stop for me.

One of the first was Matthew Morrison, who was just breaking out on *Glee*. He saw my sign, and even though his publicist was yanking him into the event, he insisted on coming over because he loved the show so much. That was always fun—the celebrities who stopped seemed so happy to see me, and they raved about how much they adored Howard.

At the *Sex and the City 2* premiere, I was once again stuck way in the back of the red carpet when I saw Sarah Jessica Parker making her way down the line, about twenty yards away from me. I knew at that rate there was no way I would get anywhere near her. Meanwhile, I was immobilized behind the metal police barrier and there was security everywhere, not to mention so many people between me and Sarah that reaching her would be like shoving from one end to the other of a rush-hour subway car. But screw that. I was going to interview Sarah Jessica Parker if it was the last thing I did. Since I was at the very back, I managed to squeeze around the spot where the barrier met the entrance. With my VIP pass I knew that no one would think I was a petite, blond assassin, but still I was not where I should have been, and at minimum I was risking being decapitated by one of those crazy-long camera booms. I shouldered my way through the line, and just as Sarah was being ushered away by her publicists, thank God she saw me—and heard me screaming. She stopped, her face lit up, and she said, "Oh my God, I love Howard! Please tell him I said hello and I think he's a genius!" She could not have been nicer or sweeter, and in the ten or fifteen seconds that I managed to get with her before her publicist physically dragged her way, she gave me exactly what I needed. Bless her heart. Celebrities like Sarah were shocked to see the *Howard Stern Show* reporter shoved to the back of the line—and they genuinely seemed concerned for me, like they would have invited me in and given me a cup of soup if they could have.

Hands down, the best red-carpet experience I ever had was at the premiere of *Dinner for Schmucks*. Paramount gave the show its very own platform at the end of the red carpet, so for the first time ever the celebrities were actually *lining up* to be interviewed by me. It was amazing, and all because of their respect for Howard Stern. Steve Carell stood next to me chatting away, and Zach Galifianakis is such a huge Stern fan that I think he would have stayed there all night. The only downside was that it was an incredibly hot and humid summer evening and my hair got frizzier by the minute.

As ferocious as I can be on the red carpet, I've settled down a lot in my personal life. My coworkers can't believe it when I tell them what a wild child I used to be. They know me only as I am now, so they think I'm such a homebody—like all I do after work is go home, play with my cat, and practice my violin. And, yeah, sometimes that's exactly what I do.

Now I play with a chamber group, and we give performances at the end of every semester. Once I was walking along to my performance with my violin tucked under my arm and a stranger asked me if I played for the Philharmonic. I smiled and said, "Why, yes, I do!" I let a few seconds pass before I admitted that no, I did not actually play for the symphony orchestra. But I loved that she made that mistake; I guess I carry my violin with a certain professionalism. I do practice every day, and not always because I want to. Sometimes I don't really feel like it, but I practice anyway, because I don't want to let down my fellow musicians.

You can find metaphors for life anywhere—in cookie recipes, in playing with an ensemble, in homeless cats. I've found lessons in all those things and more. So I'm going to end this book with a dozen of my favorites. Some I took from my romantic relationships, some from work, some from music, and some from my friendships:

1. **Do what you love.** You'll be happier and healthier (and look younger because you won't be frowning and stressing as much).

2. **The right note at the wrong time is a wrong note (and vice versa).** There's no sense regretting the fish that got away. If he wasn't ready, or you weren't ready, the bottom line is, it wasn't the right time. And if Mr. Right comes from the weirdest place, don't get caught up in preconceived notions. Just play along.

3. **Ask questions and listen to the answers.** Especially in my romantic relationships, I was like an opera singer: me me me me me me me. It's amazing how much I learned when I stopped singing that tune.

4. **Enjoy today.** For years I was like the little kid in the backseat of the car asking "How long till we get there?" every five minutes. Just recently I looked at my eighty-

eight-year-old father and I realized how quickly time passes. Now I try to appreciate the ride and not always calculate the distance yet to travel.

5. **It's okay to cry over a job.** If you follow mantra number one, then you already do what you love. So of course you're going to be sad when it ends. There's not a thing wrong with that. Now go find another job you love.

6. **Titles are earned, not granted.** Respect and love come from how you behave, not what you're called.

7. **Let them fall in love with you first.** In my life, I've done lots of tryouts for jobs. It's hard to think, *Oh my God, I just have to get this job,* without projecting all kinds of desperation. Instead, tell yourself to take things one project at a time. Do the best job you can as you go along, rather than obsessing over the big prize. The same goes for romance—don't go into a first date thinking, *Oh my God, I hope this is my next boyfriend.* Instead think, *Let's have a nice evening.* One date at a time.

8. **Don't shoot from the hip.** Slow and steady wins the race. I've seen too many people grab at the first shiny object they saw—the big-paying job that was too good to be true, for example—and before they knew it, they were out of work or their show was canceled.

9. **Nice people know nice people.** You can really judge a person by the kind of people they attract to them. Kind people draw other kind people to them. Similarly, if your new friend or boyfriend is surrounded by jerks, you might want to think twice.

10. **It all trickles down from the top.** Same idea—if

the big boss is a maniac, chances are there is some dysfunction in that organization. And if your new boyfriend seems to have drama in every quarter of his life—from work to friends to family—then chances are you're going to end up being part of the drama.

11. **Strike while the iron is cool.** It took me a long time to figure this one out. It's so easy to yell or get upset at someone (or something) when emotions are running high. Better to take a walk or sleep on a situation before blurting something out you didn't mean to say. Also, people will be more likely to hear what you're saying if you're calm, rather than screaming at them.

12. **Learn to like the word *okay*.** Everything doesn't have to be brilliantly stupendous all the time. When everything's okay, then that's all right.

I'm not promising that if you follow all these mantras, your life will be perfect. Mine definitely isn't. But who wants to be perfect? Perfect is boring. Boring is absolute death on the radio, and it's no fun in life, either. I'd rather fall on my face once in a while than never to take a step up (or down). Accidents will happen when I'm taking chances, and usually the scrapes are minor. I just dust myself off and keep going. Because the reward of finding something amazing just around the next corner is way too irresistible to pass up.

This is a very easy cookie recipe to make and remember. I call it the 1, 2, 3 recipe. 1 cup sugar, 1 cup butter, 1 egg, 2 teaspoons vanilla, 3 cups flour. After all I went through to feel good about myself, I wanted something very easy and delicious to be the last cookie in the book. It's a back-to-basics kind of recipe. But just because it's straightforward doesn't mean it's boring—God forbid. What is richer and more satisfying than butter, sugar, and vanilla? With such wonderful ingredients, there's really no need to further complicate things. Another lesson learned.

SUGAR COOKIES

1 cup (2 sticks) unsalted butter, at
   room temperature
1 cup sugar
1 egg
2 teaspoons vanilla
3 cups all-purpose flour

1 egg (for egg wash)
2½-inch round cookie cutter
Sprinkles or other toppings
   (optional)

Parchment-lined baking sheets

Preheat oven to 350 degrees.

Cream butter and sugar until light and fluffy. Add egg and vanilla and mix until incorporated. Now slowly add flour until it forms a dough.

Turn out dough on floured surface and divide into two portions. Cover both in plastic wrap and chill about 20 to 30 minutes, until firm.

Roll out to ¼-inch thickness on floured surface. Using 2½-inch round cookie cutter, cut out cookies and place on parchment-lined cookie sheet with a metal cookie spatula, spacing cookies an inch apart.

Beat remaining egg, in a small dish. Brush beaten egg wash on cookies, adding sprinkles (or whatever toppings you like).

Gather up scraps of cookies and roll out again. If cookie dough gets too soft, rechill.

Bake 12 to 15 minutes. Do not overcook. They should be done when they puff and look set.

Cool cookies on rack.

If you want to ice the cookies, skip the egg wash and ice cookies when completely cooled.

Makes about 47 cookies.

(OR, HOW YOU TOO CAN BE A COOKIE-PARTY-THROWING GODDESS)

I'm not going to tell you that you have to have a cookie party in order to be happy, but for me it was a big milestone along the way, so I decided to leave you with my best advice for how to throw a party of your own. Does your party have to revolve around cookies? No. Does pretty much everyone love cookies? Yes. And I think that says it all. You could pick a different theme for your next party, but why would you want to?

I'm no Emily Post. Or Martha Stewart. I don't turn up my nose at paper napkins. And I'm not a food snob, either, so I'm not going to send you in search of organic, locally produced flour or tell you to grind your own spices. The only hard-and-fast rule here is that the cookies at your party must be homemade.

You don't have to make them all yourself—you can have friends bring some—but the cookies must be made by someone you know (and, no, that nice guy at the local bakery does not count). One year a coworker's mother's manicurist made cookies. And they were amazing! He didn't try to pass them off as his own, and he was happy to brag about her skills. A year before I had started giving out blue ribbons to the best cookie of the evening (I enlisted a panel of friends to judge), and the manicurist's cookies won that year. They *were* homemade, after all, and by very well-maintained hands.

So it's absolutely fine to invite cookie donations, but I think the lion's share of the cookies should come from your own kitchen. How you serve them is totally up to you, though. If you want to serve all those homemade cookies on paper towels or old newspaper, I really don't care. In fact, the best parties I've ever been to have been the least formal. I have fond memories of my mother's friends coming over for bridge or mah-jongg, and my mother filling bowls with chocolate licorice and setting out some grocery store cheese and crackers on a tray. It wasn't fancy, but it was fun, and it felt special to me and to her friends. My cookie parties are my version of my mother's bridge and chocolate licorice. The only difference is that I serve way more booze.

IT ALWAYS MAKES ME laugh when I open up a magazine about cooking for a crowd and the home kitchen in the picture is the size of my entire apartment. What's to complain about if you have at least two ovens and a second freezer in the basement? When you live in an apartment with a kitchen the size of a restaurant bathroom, you have to be a lot more creative, and advance preparation is key. But don't let the size of your kitchen (or your apartment) scare you away from having a party. If I can do it, you can do it. Here's a picture of my own galley kitchen to prove that I'm not secretly in possession of a magazine-worthy spread.

If, like me, you have just one refrigerator and freezer, then I definitely recommend that you eat up the contents of your freezer in the weeks leading up to your party, because your freezer is going to become your best friend. It's where you're going to store your chocolate chip cheesecake squares (recipe on page 106) and all the cookie dough that you're going to mix up in advance.

One of the nice things about cookies is that they're not really attached to any particular season. Sure, everyone thinks of cookies at Christmas, so a holiday party is a no-brainer, but I also like throwing cookie parties in the fall, right when the weather is starting to get crisp. And there's no reason you can't have one in the spring or even in the summer (you can give your friends an excuse not to skip town for the beach). And because cookies can be baked at least a day in advance (and bar cookies can be baked and frozen even further in advance), you don't have to worry about heating up your house or apartment on the day of the party. Just add some nice, cold champagne, and a selection of wines and soft drinks, and you're good to go for any time of year. It's up to you if you want to decorate with fresh flowers, fall leaves, or evergreen.

Truth be told, I'm not big on decorating, but when I first started working in TV, the stylist I hired to help me figure out how to dress for the camera also offered to decorate my cookie parties for me. It was amazing what he did with some brown butcher paper. He crumpled it so that it had the texture of old parchment and covered my dinner table with it, which looked like a million bucks. In the fall he hung it on the walls and created fall foliage out of more paper and raffia. At one of my holiday parties he hung icicles all over the apartment. If decorating is your thing, then maybe you don't need someone like him, but if you're like me, then my advice is to grab a stylish friend and put him or her to work so you can focus on other things. And remember that as long as your bathroom is clean, most guests care way more about what they eat and drink than what's hanging on the walls.

That's the general stuff. Now let's break things down.

THE INVITE LIST

A fun party is a crowded party. I don't want to be able to see the floor when I'm having a party. So when you're thinking of making your invite list, don't think about how many people you can comfortably fit in your space—think about how many people you can *uncomfortably* fit in there. And remember that not everyone is going to come at the same time.

My friends make fun of me for inviting every new person I meet to my next cookie party, but my approach makes for a great mix of people. I never know who's going to walk through my door (including Tony Soprano). If you aren't the type to invite every stranger you encounter, that's okay, but definitely give your guests the option of bringing a plus-one. That way you'll meet some new people, and your guests will too.

E-mail your invites about five weeks in advance of the party, and then do a follow-up reminder e-mail about two and a half weeks before. You definitely don't have to get fancy with the invite, but I think it's fun to throw in a picture and get clever with your subject line so people start getting excited in advance. When I was flipping through a teen magazine for work a number of years ago, I spotted some illustrations that I really liked, so I asked the editor there if I could hire the artist to do some work for me. It turned out that the artist was actually a teenaged reader named Hannah Alexander. I ended up hiring her to work on my website and to do a bunch of my cookie party invites. Here's one of my favorites, with me and Lucky:

WHAT (AND HOW MUCH) TO SERVE TO EAT

Just remember: this is a cookie party. So you can serve bar cookies and brownies, but if the dessert requires a fork, don't serve it. I've also found that fresh fruit desserts are tricky. And if you put together fresh fruit with something that needs to be sliced and then eaten with a fork, I'm afraid that's a no go. I've had guests bring fresh fruit tarts that were absolutely gorgeous, but for some mysterious reason they weren't gobbled up. In my experience it's much safer to stick with rich, satisfying cookies and bar cookies that are easy to eat and require only fingers.

Look at the yield of all your recipes (and make sure you follow the directions for how big or small to make the cookies so that you don't end up with far fewer cookies than you expected). Figure that at least half your guests will bring someone if you've given them the option. Now calculate how many guests you're likely to have and figure that you'll want to allow for about five cookies per person. Then I always make a few extra batches—trust me, you will not believe how many cookies adults can devour. My standby for backups is my trusty chocolate chip cheesecake bars because I can serve them right out of the freezer.

When you're figuring out what cookies to serve, consider your invite list. I've observed that men love chocolate and peanut butter, so they love anything chocolate, anything peanut butter, and anything chocolate with peanut butter. Or peanut butter with chocolate. At the risk of generalizing, I will say that women can be a little trickier. There are women who aren't afraid to eat and like everything, and obviously they're the easiest and most appreciative. Then there are women who don't want to reveal in public that they like cookies. For these women (and some more rigorously health-conscious men), the oatmeal cookie was invented. The truth is that oatmeal cookies are no lower in calories or fat and sugar than anything else, but people convince themselves that oatmeal as an ingredient makes the cookies healthy. Finally, there is one sure bet that's a hit with everyone, male or female: brownies.

One last note: no matter what you make, if you take my advice to keep the serving size small, then your guests will actually end up eating more.

WHAT (AND HOW MUCH) TO SERVE TO DRINK

I've tried serving mixed drinks in the past, but then I found them to be a big headache. So now I just serve champagne and wine. I always start out with one bottle per four to six people that I've invited. Guests will bring more, and I've never run out of alcohol. I also provide soft drinks and lots of ice, because sugar can make you thirsty. And in case someone brings a bottle of vodka or other liquor, I have some orange juice and cranberry juice for mixing. One year a coworker brought a few cartons of eggnog and it was such a hit that I've served it every year since.

THE COUNTDOWN TO THE PARTY

One of the hardest things about entertaining is making sure everything is prepared and baked on time. Thankfully cookies are sturdy and you can bake them in advance. And there's lots of other preparation you can do in advance as well. You'll still be frantic the day of your party, but at least you'll be organized.

5 weeks before . . .

- **Make your grocery list and purchase as much as possible**. As soon as you've sent your invites, collected all your recipes, and calculated how much booze you need, you can start buying what you need. Anything nonperishable can be purchased way in advance, and butter and eggs last a long time, too, so if you've got the time, go ahead and buy everything you can (and have room to store).
- **Make a list of supplies, and check that you have everything you need.** I buy many of my supplies at a baking supply store. If you don't have one in your town, check the web. I've also had great luck at department stores and big box stores. Here's a list of what I recommend having in your arsenal:

1. A set of **mixing bowls**.

2. A good **rubber spatula** for scraping out bowls.

3. A nice, **thin spatula** for lifting cookies off trays (the thinner the better).

4. **Ice cream scoops,** for scooping drop cookies. I use a ⅜-ounce scoop most often, but for a few recipes in this chapter I use a ⅞-ounce scoop.

5. **Cookie sheets**. If your oven is wide enough to hold two cookie sheets side by side, then you should have four cookie sheets so that you can always have two ready to go with uncooked cookies when the baked ones come out. I like having a mix of cookie sheets—full sized and half sized. I love the half-sized sheets for the remaining dough that won't fill up a whole sheet.

6. **Baking pans**. For bar cookies and brownies, I recommend having a few sets of 9 x 13-inch pans. As with the cookie sheets, if you can fit two pans side by side in your oven, then have four of them if possible. This saves a lot of time. Remember, you can always borrow from friends. I like metal pans—preferably dark—with straight sides and sharp corners. For the life of me I don't know who invented pans with curved edges—they're the worst.

7. **Mixer**. You don't have to have an expensive standing mixer in order to have a cookie party (although if you do have one, that's great, and if you can borrow one, that's great too). A hand mixer with a strong motor should tackle any recipe in this book. That said, if you can save up and buy your own standing mixer, I think it's an excellent investment. It will make baking so much more enjoyable. I

bought mine from a neighbor who was moving to France. He didn't want to lug it to Europe, so I got a great deal. I love it, and I think it looks beautiful in my kitchen. I affectionately wipe it down after each recipe—it's one of my most prized possessions.

8. **Parchment paper**. Lots and lots of it. I adore the stuff, and I share that love with all the pastry chefs I've ever known. However, I'm not a fan of the rolled parchment paper you can find in the supermarket. It's always curling up and it never tears cleanly. I buy precut cookie-tray-sized sheets from a cooking supply store on the web. The sheets come lying flat, so they're much easier to work with. You'll notice that for bar cookies I always recommend lining the pan with parchment paper, with a few inches overhanging each of the short sides. This way you can use those extra few inches of paper like a handle to lift the entire recipe out of the pan. It's so much easier than buttering a pan and worrying about messing things up while you try to dig them out with a spatula. Parchment paper is just as great for lifting cookies off trays. Alfred Stephens taught me this trick that I use to this day—it's like magic, similar to pulling a tablecloth off a table fast without having anything spill: once the cookies were cooled a bit on a large cookie sheet, he'd take the edge of the parchment paper and quickly pull it (and the cookies) off the tray. It made a sound like *wissshhh.* The cookies amazingly stayed on the parchment paper and then he could quickly reuse the cookie sheet for another batch. He kept repeating this until he had stacks of cookies. It made the process very fast and efficient. (One

note of caution: while learning this, expect some cookies to hit the floor.)

9. **Self-sealing plastic bags, cellophane, and foil**. For wrapping and freezing cookie dough and already baked bars.

10. **Foldable cooling racks**. If you have a lot of baked goods cooling at once you can spread these anywhere— dining table, coffee table, wherever you've got surface area (you'll need it).

11. **Plastic serving trays**. You can get these at a good stationery or party supply store.

12. **Placecards and toothpicks**. For writing the names of cookies and labeling trays. (More on this below.)

13. **Paper bakery boxes**. This is the best way of storing drop cookies once you've baked them. I'm not a fan of plastic containers, because I find that storing in plastic can affect the texture of baked goods. But if you have them, by all means use them. They work just fine.

14. **Paper plates and napkins**. Don't even think about washing dishes.

15. **Plastic glassware**. Ditto. And I have to add that I know the tall red 12-ounce plastic cups are all the rage, but I think the clear 6-ounce glasses are classier.

16. **Plastic goodie bags**. For sending cookies home with guests at the end of the night. This way, no leftovers! Around the holidays you can find decorated plastic zipper bags, which are a cute way of sending home goodies.

3 weeks before . . .

Bake and freeze bar cookies. People are often surprised
how far in advance I make them, but it's so great (and
calming) to get these out of the way, and they freeze really
well. The key to freezing bar cookies is to cool them, then
refrigerate them until they're very firm. Then you can slice
them, carefully remove them from the pan (lifting up by the
short edges of the parchment paper that you've used to
line the pan) and freeze them wrapped in a double layer of
cellophane and foil.

2 weeks before . . .

- **Mix and freeze drop cookie batter** in plastic zipper
  bags. Be sure to label them.
- **Mix, roll out, and freeze rolled-out cookie dough**
  (such as the gingerbread men on page 69). Once
  you've rolled out the dough, you can lay it flat between
  sheets of parchment paper, then wrap it in a double
  layer of cellophane and foil and freeze flat.

1 week before . . .

Make cookie labels. Get those placecards you bought
and write the names of all the cookies and bars you're
making, then attach each one to a toothpick with a little
tape. Be sure to leave some of these blank just in case your
guests bring some cookies that you'd like to label.

3 days before . . .

Thaw drop cookie batter.

2 days before . . .

- **Bake drop cookies,** cool on racks, and store between layers of parchment paper in paper bakery boxes, or plastic containers. Store in the fridge if you have room, or in the coolest, driest place in your home. I've even stored cookies on the inside ledge of a window, with the window slightly cracked—instant refrigeration in the colder months.
- **Thaw rolled-out cookie dough.**

1 day before . . .

- **Cut and bake rolled-out cookie dough**. Store between layers of parchment paper in paper bakery boxes or plastic containers. Can be left in a cool dry place until you're ready to put out for the party.
- **Clean and decorate** (if you like).

Morning of the party . . .

- **Thaw all the bar cookies** you made, except for the chocolate chip cheesecake bars—those can stay frozen until you're ready to serve them.
- **Chill booze and drinks.** If there's not enough room

in your fridge (there's never enough in mine), you can use a cooler that you already own, or buy several Styrofoam box coolers and fill them with ice. Keep them near the bar so that guests can help themselves.

- **Roll up rugs and move out as much furniture as possible** (see more about seating later in the chapter).
- **Clear surfaces** where you'll be serving food and drinks.
- **Create layering foundations on serving tables**. You want some trays to be high and some to be low. This creates visual interest. You can even turn over a bowl and set a tray on top. I've also used an empty glass hurricane lamp, filling it full of cookies (sturdy ones are best for this). Get creative.
- **Put out napkins, plates, and plastic cups.**

1 hour before the party . . .

- **Arrange the first round of cookies**. Place cookies on trays, poke a label into one cookie or bar on each.
- **Assemble the bar**. I use a rolling cart from my kitchen.
- **Light candles**. I love scented candles, particularly at the holidays. My favorites are from the Gap and Nest. They really remind me of what a Vermont inn smells like. Your guests will love the smell, too. Cinnamon or pumpkin spice scents are great for fall parties.
- **Have a drink.** You need it.

PARTY 101

Throwing a great party is more art than science and sometimes it's hard to figure out why one party is amazing and another is a flop. But I've figured out a few strategies for stacking the odds in your favor:

1. **Timing is everything**. I always call the party for 8 P.M. and I know the first person will arrive at 8:30 P.M. It's nice to have a few close friends promise to get there on the dot, just so you're not panicking in an empty apartment. Every party has its own rhythm and there's going to be an ebb and flow, so don't get anxious if it feels like the energy is starting to flag (for more on how to keep the energy up, read on). Expect the prime time of the party will be 9:00 to 10:30 P.M. and then the last guests will likely leave around midnight—and those will be your closest friends and/or the person you're having sex with. I've never had to kick anyone out, but I remember once I was sweeping the floor at 12:30 A.M. and someone actually rang the bell. I gave them some leftover cookies and sent them on their way.

2. **Music**. I used to always start out with slow R&B, and then I'd move on to some more up-tempo stuff as the evening went on. You know the tastes (and age group) of the crowd you've invited, so it's fun to throw in something nostalgic—Michael Jackson never fails. Now that I work in satellite radio, I don't bother with CDs or a playlist, I just turn on SiriusXM. You can't go wrong with its music channels, and there are hundreds to pick from. Sirius XM

even has annual Christmas-themed channels. Just stay tuned to the energy level in the room. If it's still early in the party and things are starting to drag, pick up the beat. If it's later in the party and things are starting to mellow, then it's fine to keep it that way.

3. **No sitting down**. Unless there's a reason certain people would have a tough time standing, I try to get as much seating out of my apartment as possible. You want people moving and circulating, not plopping themselves down, glued to one spot. I've actually moved furniture into neighbors' apartments (and rugs, too, because a wooden floor is a lot easier to clean than a carpet).

4. **No clumping**. The best parties offer a mix of people who don't all know one another. And I feel like it's my job as hostess to introduce different groups of people to each other. Otherwise, you end up with a party where everyone is attached with Velcro to the one or two people they know, like it's the first day of school. I get a lot of pleasure from figuring out who would love to meet each other. Maybe this person works in print media and that one works in radio and I think they'd like comparing notes. Maybe this person is a marathoner and that one is a cyclist. Maybe she's a dog lover and he's a vet. I have spent whole parties dragging my guests around meeting each other—I will actually take them by the hand and pull them away from whatever security blanket they've attached themselves to. Don't be shy about it. This is your job, and everyone will have more fun this way—and they'll thank you for it later. Because when that dog lover has a problem with her best

friend, who do you think she's going to call? Introducing people is my way of giving back to the people I love.

5. **Always keep lipstick nearby**. Touch-ups are important when you're running yourself ragged while being a social butterfly.

6. **Make sure your air-conditioning works** if the temperature outside is warmer than 75. If it's a good party, then it's crowded, and it will be hot. Even in the winter, packed parties can get steamy. One year, in the dead of winter, my air-conditioning was on the fritz and people were sweating. It's no fun to see your male friends' dress shirts sticking to their bodies like they just ran a few laps. It's a cookie marathon you're throwing, not an actual road race.

7. **Make sure your neighbors know you're having a party,** and if you like them (or don't actively dislike them), then invite them. Either way, make sure to warn them about your party in advance. Then they won't complain.

8. **Seek help!** You don't have to do everything yourself. If guests ask if they can bring anything, don't be shy—say yes. And don't hesitate to be specific so you get what you need instead of duplicates of what you don't. I've never seen wine go to waste, so you can always ask for a few backups. You can ask friends to bring their favorite cookies, too. If you know you've got plenty of chocolate chip cookies made, give them an idea of what kind of cookie would really add to the array. Even if the cookies your guests bring aren't all equally great, you can put them out at the end of the night when your guests are too well lubricated to care. You

can also enlist some extra sets of hands at the party. When I realized that I was too busy shuttling cookies back and forth from the kitchen to enjoy my guests, Joan Hamburg of WOR Radio gave me the brilliant advice to hire a few students from the Columbia University Bartending School. I have them come early, show them where everything is, and then they can refill platters and restock the bar. It's amazing help and worth every penny (and it's really not that expensive). Plus, if you still have any cookies or brownies left over at the end of the night, they'll be more than happy to take them off your hands.

WHEN MY GUESTS ARRIVE, usually the first thing they say to me is, "Where's Lucky?" He's the real celebrity at my parties. But forget it, Lucky makes a quick disappearing act before the doorbell even rings. He knows what's good for him and he stays well hidden until about 11:30, when he emerges to take a star turn for the few remaining guests.

And it's not just cats that can get shell-shocked by entertaining. At a certain point—it might be the stroke of midnight, or it might be 5 A.M. the next morning or 12:30 the next afternoon—you will look around your post-cookie-party home and you will ask yourself what the heck you were thinking. You'll find your own cat (or your dog, or your boyfriend) cowering under the bed, and he will be wondering the same thing.

Then, you'll clean up the mess, get over the trauma, and you'll want to do the whole thing again next year—and do it even better. Chocolate stains are temporary, wine stains less so, but the memories of your cookie party are forever.

I know people who refuse to serve red wine at their parties just to avoid the mess, but that's not who I am. I'd rather stock up on club soda and salt than tell my guests they can't drink something that stains. Over the years, I've had maybe one really bad carpet stain that I had to call in professionals to deal with, and that's not so bad.

Just accept in advance that you'll find a cookie ground into a spot in your apartment that you never would have expected. After the last guest leaves (and preferably with the help of a friend), sweep up the worst of it, and collect dirty plates, cups, and all food scraps into bags. You don't have to clean everything, because you really want to crash at this point, but you do want to get rid of anything that smells or you might step in on your way to the bathroom in the middle of the night. Finally, take all that trash out of the apart-ment so you don't have to smell it the next morning.

The next day—after you've had a cup of coffee—you can deal with the rest. And you can enjoy all the e-mails and texts and tweets and Facebook wall posts you get from people who loved your party. Despite all the hard work, you might even find yourself suffering from a bout of PCPS (post-cookie-party syndrome). I know I always do. A good antidote is to pack up any leftovers and take them into work Monday morning. Then you can soak up a few more compliments.

THERE ISN'T A WRONG cookie to make for a cookie party, but here are some more party-tested winners that I guarantee will make your guests happy. And if you're a newbie baker, my best advice is: don't worry. It's very hard to go wrong with butter and sugar— and chocolate and peanut butter. If you make sure your invite list is diverse and your bar is well stocked, you could serve cookies made of flavored Styrofoam and your guests would still walk away happy.

MINI APPLE PIES

When I first started throwing cookie parties, I tried serving full-sized cakes and pies, but they were never as popular as the cookies. It's just too hard to hold a drink in one hand and try to eat something with a fork with the other hand. And once you start cutting into a pie, it stops looking nice on the table, so the whole display can become an unappetizing mess. The solution? Mini apple pies. My guests love these, and they're one of my favorite recipes. They're just as delicious at room temperature, but if you have time before the party starts, you can pop these into a 325-degree oven for about 10 minutes to warm them up. They smell amazing.

2 ready-made piecrusts

For the apple filling:
2 Granny Smith apples, peeled and diced
1½ tablespoons sugar
¼ teaspoon ground cinnamon

For the strudel topping:

⅓ cup butter (cold)

⅓ cup flour

¼ cup sugar

¼ cup brown sugar

1½ teaspoons cinnamon

2½-inch round cookie cutter

Minimuffin pan

Preheat oven to 350 degrees.

Using the 2½-inch round cookie cutter, cut out 24 circles to form mini-piecrusts. Place one circle in each well of a minimuffin pan, and push dough down, forming a cup shape.

In a bowl, toss together diced apples, sugar, and cinnamon until apples are well coated.

Fill each dough cup (two-thirds full) with apples.

In another bowl, with hands (my preferred method) or a pastry cutter, smush together butter, flour, sugars, and cinnamon to form a strudel. Place small amount (about a teaspoon) of strudel over each mini apple pie.

Bake 15 minutes until the topping turns lightly brown. When cooled, dust with powdered sugar.

Makes 24 mini apple pies.

PLAIN-AS-BUTTER COOKIES

These cookies are so delicious, and they remind me of something important: things don't have to be complicated to be good. With so many cookies with different textures and tastes, it's nice to serve a basic butter cookie. And as any chef will tell you, it's the simple recipes that test your technique—if you can bake a butter or a sugar cookie, then you're good to go with everything else.

¾ cup (1½ sticks) unsalted butter, softened

1 cup sugar

1 egg

½ teaspoon vanilla

2 cups all-purpose flour

½ teaspoon baking powder

Parchment-lined cookie sheets

Preheat oven to 350 degrees.

Using a standing or handheld mixer, beat butter and sugar until fluffy. Scrape down sides. Add egg and vanilla. Mix until incorporated.

In separate bowl, whisk together flour and baking powder. Slowly add to butter mixture until combined.

Chill dough for about 20 minutes. This makes it easier to scoop.

Using your ⅜-ounce ice cream scoop, scoop out balls of dough and place them 2 inches apart on the parchment-lined cookie sheets. Press top of dough down gently, just a little.

Bake 11 to 13 minutes, until bottoms turn light brown. Cool on rack.

Makes about 57 small cookies.

PEPPERMINT BARK COOKIES

I started making chocolate peppermint bark bars as holiday presents for coworkers, and then I decided it would be fun to showcase the same flavors in a cookie. One look at these cookies and you'll think Christmas, and it's a nice little surprise to get the crunch of the peppermint as you bite into them.

½ cup (1 stick) unsalted butter, softened
1½ cups sugar
1 teaspoon vanilla extract
3 eggs
2 cups all-purpose flour
½ cup unsweetened cocoa powder

½ teaspoon baking soda
4 ounces semisweet chocolate chips
12 candy canes

Parchment-lined cookie sheets

Preheat oven to 325 degrees.

Cream butter and sugar. Add vanilla and eggs and mix until incorporated.

In a small bowl, sift together flour, cocoa powder, and baking soda. Add slowly to butter mixture. Scrape down the sides of the bowl.

Melt chocolate chips in a microwave in three increments of 20 seconds each. Stir between each increment until smooth and fully melted. Now mix into dough.

Place candy canes in a sealed zipper bag and crush using a meat tenderizer or a rolling pin. Stir one-third of the chopped candy canes into the dough. Place in freezer for about 10 minutes until dough is firm.

Using ⅞-ounce ice cream scoop, scoop out balls of dough, dipping tops of dough balls into remaining candy canes. Place 2 inches apart on parchment-lined cookie sheets and flatten cookies slightly.

Bake for 15 to 17 minutes until cookies are firm.

If some of the candy melts outside of cookie, wait until completely cooled; it will easily break off.

Cool on racks.

CHOCOLATE SANDWICH COOKIES
WITH VANILLA CRÈME

These are the bootleg version of an Oreo cookie, and even more delish. Some of the most popular cookies at my parties are copies of old childhood favorites. Who doesn't love chocolate mixed with vanilla and a generous heaping of nostalgia?

For the chocolate cookies:

1 cup (2 sticks) unsalted butter, softened

1 cup sugar

1 egg

1 teaspoon vanilla

2½ cups all-purpose flour

½ cup cocoa powder

For the vanilla crème:

½ cup (1 stick) unsalted butter, softened

½ cup solid vegetable shortening

3½ cups confectioners' sugar

1 tablespoon pure vanilla extract

Parchment-lined cookie sheets

2½-inch circular cookie cutter

Preheat oven to 350 degrees.

To make the cookie dough, cream butter and sugar; scrape down the sides of the bowl. Add egg and vanilla until incorporated. Add flour and cocoa powder in batches until well mixed. Make sure you scrape sides and bottom of bowl very well. Then gather the dough into a ball and divide in half, flattening into two disks. Place each disk between sheets of parchment paper and roll to ¼-inch thickness. Freeze flat for about 10 minutes, until dough is firm.

Using cookie cutter, cut out circle shapes in the dough and place on a parchment-lined cookie sheet, about 1 inch apart. Bake for about 12 to 13 minutes. Cookies should be firm and start to turn a little bit darker.

Cool on wire racks.

To prepare the vanilla crème, cream together all the ingredients until smooth and spreadable.

Turn half the cookies over, so the flatter side is facing up. These will be the bottoms. Place 1 tablespoon of crème in the center of each bottom half. Spread out to edges. Place one cookie top on each, so the slightly domed side is facing up. Press slightly.

Makes 20 sandwich cookies.

THANKFUL COOKIES

These are my favorite cookies for the fall, and I especially love baking them for Thanksgiving. The hint of orange with the oatmeal is a sure hit. My father especially loves these. When he's visiting from Florida, I always pack him a box to take back, but they never make it to the plane.

¾ cup (1½ sticks) unsalted butter, softened

⅞ cup packed brown sugar

1 egg

¾ tablespoon honey

1 teaspoon vanilla

1 cup all-purpose flour

8 ounces old-fashioned oats (not instant)

6 ounces fresh cranberries, chopped (or half of a 12-ounce bag)

Zest of one large orange

Parchment-lined cookie sheets

⅞-ounce ice cream scoop

Preheat oven to 350 degrees.

Cream butter and sugar until fluffy. Scrape down the bowl. Beat in egg, honey, and vanilla.

Add flour and mix until well incorporated. Stir in oats, then cranberries and orange zest. Mix well.

Using your ⅞-ounce ice cream scoop, scoop out balls of dough and place on parchment-lined cookie sheet 1½ inches apart. Press slightly.

Bake 15 to 20 minutes. Cookies should be firm.

Cool on wire racks.

Makes 25 cookies.

GREEN TEA SHORTBREAD COOKIES

These have a delicious, subtle flavor, and their pale green color is really lovely. These are also good for those health-conscious guests who think that anything green (and green tea) must be healthy. Just don't tell them about all the butter. Note: you can find green tea powder in health food stores and even some larger grocery stores, or online (where I've found it a little cheaper). And here's a fun fact: you can also use it for a homemade facial mask! Green tea has astringent properties and is very good for the skin—just mix it with raw egg, lemon juice, and some honey or sugar and slather it on.

1 cup (2 sticks) unsalted butter, softened

½ cup sugar

¼ teaspoon salt

2 tablespoons Matcha (green tea) powder

2¼ cups flour

Parchment-lined cookie sheets

⅞-ounce ice cream scoop

Preheat oven to 350 degrees.

In mixer, blend butter and sugar until light and fluffy. Scrape down the sides of the bowl. Add salt (it brings out the flavor of the tea, so don't skip this step). Add green tea powder. Slowly add flour until incorporated.

Make sure ingredients are mixed in well. Scrape up the bottom of bowl to make sure flour doesn't stick. This is important to make sure cookies keep their shape and don't spread during baking.

Using a ⅞-ounce ice cream scoop, scoop out balls of dough and place 2 inches apart on a parchment-lined cookie sheet. Balls should look like light green scoops of butter.

Bake for 15 to 18 minutes, until cookies are light brown at the edges.

Let cool completely.

When cooled pour ½ cup of confectioners' sugar in plastic or paper bag. Put cooled cookies in bag and very gently shake until cookies are completely covered with sugar.

Makes 24 cookies.

DIVA DOODLES (A.K.A. SNICKERDOODLES)

This is another simple, nostalgic cookie that never fails to please. Even though this recipe has been around forever, these cookies always bring a smile to your face. People love the chewy texture and the hint of cinnamon. And they go really nicely with wine.

½ cup (1 stick) unsalted butter, softened

¾ cup sugar

⅔ cup packed light brown sugar

1 egg

1 teaspoon vanilla extract

1 teaspoon baking powder

1½ cups all-purpose flour

½ teaspoon ground cinnamon

Parchment-lined cookie sheets

⅜-ounce ice cream scoop

For dipping:

3 tablespoons sugar

1 teaspoon cinnamon

Preheat oven to 350 degrees.

Cream butter and sugars until fluffy. Scrape down the sides of the bowl. Add egg and vanilla until incorporated.

In a small bowl, sift together baking powder, flour, and cinnamon. Slowly add to butter mixture.

In separate small bowl, mix the sugar and cinnamon for dipping.

Using ⅜-ounce ice cream scoop, scoop out dough. Dip tops of dough balls into sugar/cinnamon mix. Place dough balls on parchment-lined cookie sheets, 2½ inches apart.

Bake 10 minutes.

Cool on rack. Cookies will firm up while cooling.

Makes 50 cookies.

PEANUT BUTTER COOKIES

Peanut butter lovers are a very loyal group and if you satisfy their taste buds, they'll be your devoted fans for life. This is a classic recipe that never fails to please. You can add chocolate chips to them and skip the cross-hatching, but I love the pure peanut flavor of the old-fashioned, unadulterated way.

½ cup (1 stick) unsalted butter, softened
1 cup packed light brown sugar
1 large egg
1 teaspoon vanilla extract
1 cup smooth (not natural) peanut butter

1½ cups all-purpose flour
1 teaspoon baking soda

Parchment-lined cookie sheets
⅞-ounce ice cream scoop

Preheat oven to 350 degrees.

Cream butter and sugar in bowl until fluffy. Scrape down the sides of the bowl. Add egg and vanilla until incorporated. Add peanut butter. Mix until well blended.

In a small bowl, sift together flour and baking soda. Slowly add to butter mixture. Mix well. Scrape down the sides of the bowl.

Using ⅞-ounce ice cream scoop, scoop out balls of dough and place on parchment-lined cookie sheet, 2 inches apart.

Using a fork, press down on the tops of each cookie, making a crisscross pattern. The cookies will spread a little as they bake, but that's okay.

Bake for 15 to 17 minutes, until cookies firm up and start to get golden brown at the edges.

Makes about 30 cookies.

CHOCOLATE CHOW MEIN NOODLE COOKIES

*I asked my friend **Wayne Brachman** if he'd like to contribute a cookie recipe to this book, and this is the wonderful creation he came up with. Wayne is the pastry chef at Porter House in New York City, and he can whip up anything gourmet, gorgeous, and yummy at a moment's notice. He also knows how hectic life can be, so he came up with a cookie that's both tasty and easy to make. If you want something fun for Passover, substitute one cup of matzo farfel for the chow mein noodles. Just toast the farfel in a 350-degree oven for 7 minutes or until crisp.*

5 ounces semisweet, bittersweet, or white chocolate

1 five-ounce package fried chow mein noodles

¼ cup lightly toasted coconut flakes

¼ cup chopped, roasted, unsalted peanuts

¼ cup chopped dried cranberries or cherries

Parchment-lined cookie sheets

In a dry bowl, or in the top of a double boiler, melt the chocolate over barely simmering water.

Mix in the noodles, coconut, peanuts, and dried fruit. Drop walnut-sized little haystacks of the mixture onto a parchment-lined cookie sheet.

Refrigerate for 30 minutes, until set.

MUDSLIDES

*This amazing recipe comes courtesy of chocolatier **Jacques Torres**, the ultimate professional who always wears a smile on his face. I visited (and worked) in his kitchen when he was pastry* *chef at Le Cirque in New York City, and his kitchen hummed along like a well-oiled machine. Despite the demands of working in one of the top restaurants in New York City, he never let you see him sweat. It was pretty amazing watching him whip up gourmet delights like a magician, and voilà . . . a three-tiered, three-flavored mousse dessert in what seemed like seconds. Now he owns his own chain of chocolate factories and boutiques where he sells the most decadent chocolate confections, including these incredibly delicious mudslide cookies. I'm honored that he's allowing me to include the recipe here.*

1 pound 60% bittersweet
   chocolate, chopped
6 ounces unsweetened chocolate,
   chopped
½ cup plus 3 tablespoons all-
   purpose flour
2¾ teaspoons baking powder
1¼ teaspoons salt
5 large eggs, at room temperature

6 tablespoons unsalted butter, at
   room temperature
2¼ cups sugar
1 pound 60% bittersweet
   chocolate, finely chopped
1¼ cups chopped walnuts

Parchment-lined cookie sheets

Preheat the oven to 350 degrees.

Line two cookie sheets with parchment paper or silicone mats, or use nonstick pans.

Combine the 1 pound chopped bittersweet and the unsweetened chocolate in the top half of a double boiler. Place over (not touching) gently simmering water in the bottom pan and heat, stirring frequently, until completely melted. Remove from the heat and set aside.

In a bowl, stir together the flour, baking power, and salt and set aside. Crack the eggs into another bowl and set aside.

In the bowl of a stand mixer fitted with the paddle, beat the butter on medium speed until very light and fluffy. Add the sugar and beat until well blended. Add the eggs and beat just until incorporated. Then add the melted chocolate and beat to combine. On low speed, add the flour mixture a little at a time, beating after each addition until incorporated before adding more.

Remove the bowl from the mixer and fold in the finely chopped chocolate and the walnuts with a rubber spatula.

To shape the cookies, scoop out heaping tablespoonfuls of the dough, form them into balls, and place them on the prepared baking sheets, spacing the balls about 1 inch apart. Bake the cookies for about 15 minutes or until set around the edges. Remove from the oven and transfer the cookies to a wire rack to cool slightly. Serve warm.

Makes 20 large cookies.

> **Note:** Leftover cookies can be stored, airtight, at room temperature for three days or, tightly wrapped, frozen for up to one month.

NEW AGE BLACK-AND-WHITE COOKIES

*When I met **Alfred Stephens**, he was an assistant pastry chef at Bobby Flay's Mesa Grill restaurant in New York City. He was always incredibly kind and generous with his time—he certainly didn't have to spend as much time with me as he did, teaching me the tricks of his pastry trade. I am forever thankful. Not only that, he was a huge Hot 97 fan, and it was great sharing stories while we baked away early on weekend mornings. Now Alfred is a bigwig pastry chef with Todd English's organization, and once again he showed his generosity of spirit by offering me his own modern interpretation of a black-and-white cookie.*

TO MAKE THE COOKIES:

4 ounces (1 stick) of softened
  butter

⅓ cup sugar

1 teaspoon vanilla extract

¼ teaspoon lemon extract

2 eggs

1 cup plus 1 tablespoon all-
  purpose flour

2 teaspoons baking powder

1 teaspoon salt

2 tablespoons milk

2 tablespoons sour cream

2 tablespoons olive oil

Parchment-lined cookie sheets

Piping bag and tip

Preheat oven to 325 degrees.

Place the butter and sugar in the bowl of an electric mixer fitted
with a paddle attachment; beat on high speed for 2 minutes. Add
the vanilla and lemon extract, then add the eggs one at a time,
beating to incorporate between each addition.

Sift and combine the dry ingredients in a separate bowl and set
aside.

In a small bowl, mix the milk, sour cream, and olive oil until
smooth. Add the dry ingredients to the butter, sugar, and egg
mixture and mix until smooth. Add the milk mixture and mix until
that's incorporated as well.

Place the batter in a piping bag fitted with a plain piping tip. Pipe
mounds of batter—2 inches wide and 2 inches high—onto a
parchment-lined baking sheet, leaving enough space in between
for the batter to spread when baking.

Bake in a 325-degree oven for 15 minutes, turning the cookie
sheet once halfway through the baking. The cookies are done
when they are light golden brown and the centers bounce back
when touched. Remove from oven and allow to cool 1 hour.

Makes 25 large cookies.

TO MAKE THE GANACHE:

9 ounces bittersweet chocolate

1 cup heavy cream

Place the chocolate into a medium bowl. Heat the cream in a small sauce pan over high heat. Bring cream to a boil, then pour over the chopped chocolate and whisk until smooth. Let the ganache cool to room temperature.

TO MAKE THE VANILLA ICING:

1 cup water, plus 3 tablespoons
   boiling water
Pinch of salt

½ teaspoon vanilla extract
2 cups confectioners' sugar

Place the 1 cup water, salt, and vanilla extract in a small pot and bring to a boil. Place confectioners' sugar in large mixing bowl. Gradually stir in the 3 tablespoons of boiling water to the sugar to make a thick, spreadable mixture. If it's too thin add more sugar a teaspoon at a time. Place the frosting into an airtight container until you're ready to use it.

TO FROST THE COOKIES:

Hold a baked and cooled cookie in one hand and insert a small paring knife at an angle a quarter inch from the edge of the cookie. Cut a cone-shaped piece out of the center of each cookie, then fill with enough ganache until it's slightly below the lip of the cookie. Take the cone-shaped lid you just cut and trim off the pointy end so that when you place it back on the cookie you have a flat lid. Press slightly until the lid sits even. Chill the cookies in the refrigerator 30 minutes, until the ganache firms up. Remove the cookies and ice the same cored-out side of the cookie with the vanilla icing using a small offset spatula to cover up the cookie surgery.

Leave out on a wire rack for an hour so the icing firms up. Store in a clean airtight container.

Makes 8 medium-sized cookies.

You've got your practical tips and your cookie recipes, so now off you go to plan your party. First, though, one last bit of wisdom. I've been doing cookie parties for years, and still, no matter how well organized I am before, every single time I'm exhausted afterward. There's no magic wand to wave and no single piece of advice that will make it a breeze to throw a party. There will be chocolate stains somewhere in your apartment. Wine will be spilled. And you will sweat. But what I learned from entertaining people I love is the following, and these are definitely words to live by:

1. It's not about me.
2. Anything I work hard for is worth it—whether it all ends perfectly or not.

ACKNOWLEDGMENTS

I believe in keeping thank-yous brief and sincere.

First and foremost, my gratitude to Howard and Beth Stern.

The Howard 100 News Team—Brad Driver, Shuli Egar, Ralph Howard, Jon Lieberman, Michael Morales, and Steve Warren.

Robin Quivers, Fred Norris, Gary Dell'Abate, Tim Sabean, and the entire Stern staff who make waking up at 4:00 A.M. worth it. Benjy Bronk, Sal Governale, Richard Christy, Jason Kaplan, Will Murray, Jon Hein, Jamie Harmeyer, Steve Brandano, Scott Salem, Tracey Millman, Teddy Kneutter, Evan Mandelbaum. Also thanks to everyone at Howard TV.

Neil Strauss—thank you for giving me the push I needed.

Amy B.—thanks for your guidance and friendship.

Arlene, Steve, Cheryl, Nadine, and Leslie—thanks for holding on to my memories with a smile.

To Lisa Sharkey, my publisher—thank you for your vote of confidence.

My agent, Richard Abate—thank you for your creative advice.

To my co-captains—Peternelle van Arsdale, Paige Hazzan, and Amy Bendell.

To my cookie tasters: Steve Lacy, Sway, Heather B., Julio Colon, Larry Cirello, Dennis Falcone, Alexandra Di Trolio, Kid Kelly, Nicole Ryan, Rich Davis, Stanley T. Evans, Ryan Sampson, Vanessa Mojica, Julia Cunningham, Wendy Rickman, Spencer Mindich, and Geronimo.

To my former radio coworkers: Dr. Dré, Pia James, Wayne Mayo, Al Barry, Curt Flirt, Gladys Levy, John Fisher, Mary Jane Deasey, Debra Carlton, Mara Rubin, and Mark McKewen.

Chefs extraordinaire: Bobby Flay, Alfred Stephens, Wayne Brachman, Jacques Torres, and Sunny Anderson.

My chamber ensemble instructors—Mary Barto and Mara Milkis.

My Coffee Shop Crew: Adele and Judy.

To Eileen, Iris, Jeanne, and Stacy—my real-life cheerleading squad who have been there from the start.

To my cover photo shoot team: Erin McNeil/makeup and John Dallas/hair.